Beech
The fall and rise of a forest

Essays and Photographs by

AgathaO

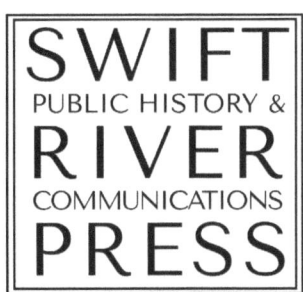

SWIFT
PUBLIC HISTORY &
RIVER
COMMUNICATIONS
PRESS

Published by Swift River Press. All rights reserved. No portion of this book may be reproduced in any form without permission from the author, except as permitted by U.S. copyright law. Request photo reproduction permissions through *swiftriverpress.com*.

ISBN: 978-0-9989611-1-8

Nature is, above all, profligate. Don't believe them when they tell you how economical and thrifty nature is, whose leaves return to the soil. Wouldn't it be cheaper to leave them on the tree in the first place? This deciduous business alone is a radical scheme, the brainchild of a deranged manic-depressive with limitless capital. Extravagance! Nature will try anything once.

— Annie Dillard, *Pilgrim at Tinker Creek*

CONTENTS

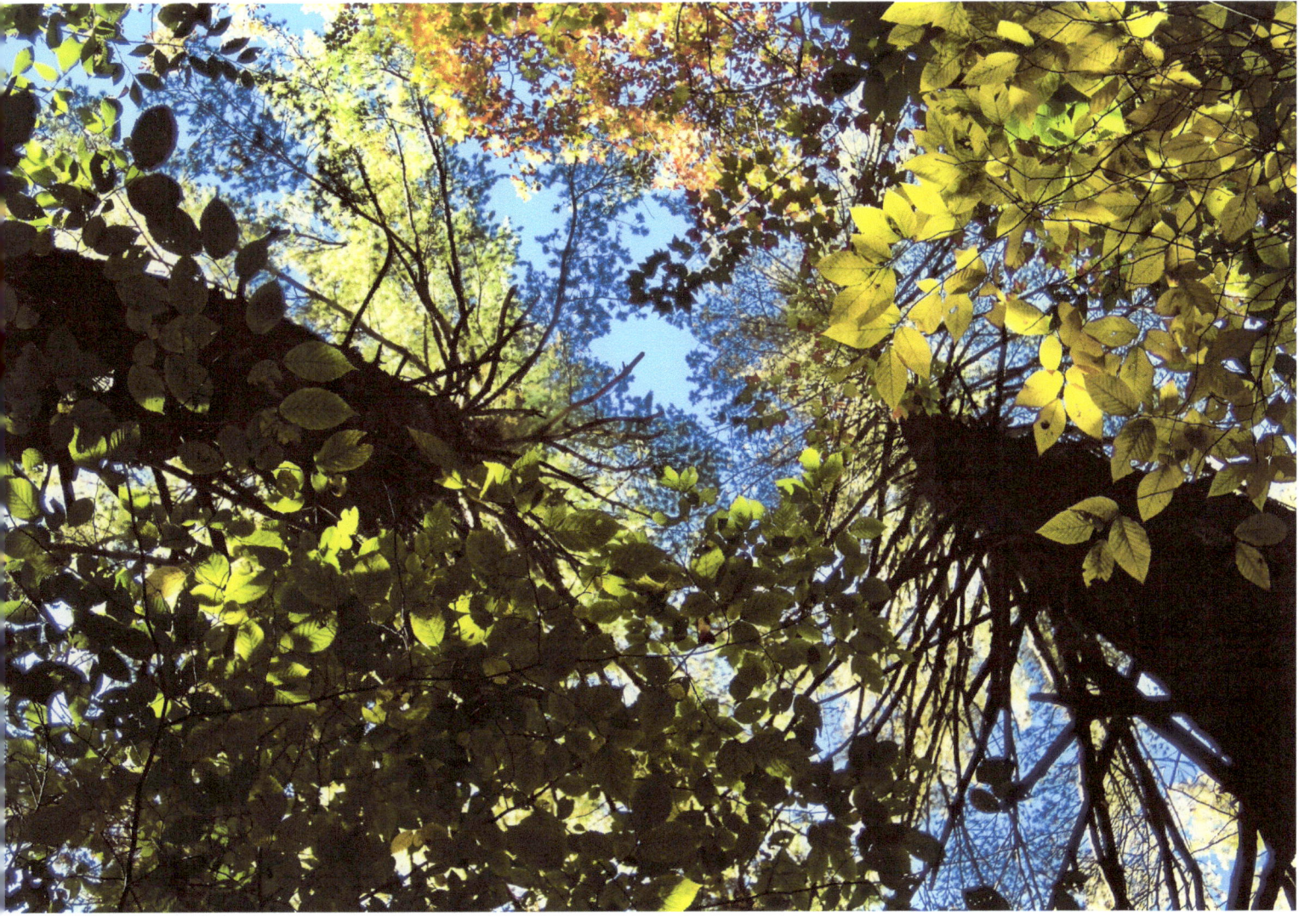

I sniff the air deeply, but what is my nose compared to that of the hound, bounding though hill and dale, in hot pursuit of the uncatchable?

Still, a clumsy dame can walk though a forest every day and have it be the world to her — a world of joy, sadness, full of longing and homecoming — cursing as she stumbles into an Agatha trap, laughing madly as she scrambles up.

To be free to fall, get dirty, get up, walk this way and that, and at every turn be reminded of an entire world that exists just for itself, fragrant, smelly, gorgeous in all its ways, that is happiness.

Walking through the forest, I am transported.

How did it get here? No one tells a beech to grow here, a maple there. No architect designed the pattern that is followed — not in my world, in any case. And a forest without an architect is that much more exciting to be in, if you think about it.

The forest is endless variation on a pattern, an endless combination of physics, chemistry, biology, and chance. The forest is a miracle of biological collaboration.

Here and there you'll find a bit of human intervention mixed in, but you can't even call that architecture for it's gone wild. Barberries, prickly nasties with pretty red berries that farmers planted to keep their gardens safe from predation; daylilies, native to Asia, that once graced otherwise stark farmyards; the absence of signature species like stately chestnuts and beeches.

These signs, and the pervasive architecture of stone walls and cellar holes remind me that once upon a time this forest was gone in most of New England

Gone.

Colonial settlement spelled the doom of the vast New England forests, and deforestation continued with a vengeance after independence from old England.

A map of 1830 Plainfield will show you where the trees from the old forest still stood. It has many mills but not too many trees. Fewer, perhaps, than in many older suburbs today. Even then, the people knew the mills themselves were doomed to follow their fodder into never-never land, why else map the trees?

With the mills gone, the forest is back. It has changed, yes, but it's back as a forest: a self-perpetuating organism that spans an entire region.

When the forest was first cleared around here — just before the Revolution this was — beeches were stacked like so many match sticks in grand piles to be lit and make potash.

It was said that, if you looked up the hill from Williamsburg, all you saw was a red glow though fog. Smoke and fire everywhere, men in managing giant piles of smoldering logs with long sticks. Hell had come to the hills.*

From the hills' perspective in any case. But the trees had a life force that outlasted the economic calculations of men.

Until now.

For years, no one cared about our forests, as they slowly reclaimed land that had been cleared for farming and the manufacture of broom handles. Sections were cut for firewood and then left to grow again. Few people lived here, and late twentieth-century settlers dribbling in were not all that inclined to tackle whole acreages of white pines, maples, and birches with some other stuff mixed in like black cherry.

But now our forest has been rediscovered. Biomass plants, pulp plants, solar farms, and the odd windmill vie for our wood or our space, or both. Clearing can be made to pay in the name of renewable energy. The *clear and replace* calculation from two hundred years ago is going strong.

Our future-oriented but still shortsighted mechanistic laws seem to make no distinction between solar farms built on a parking lot or brown-site versus solar farms built on top of a slaughtering of the trees.

It makes me heartsick. Even what we thought were the best of environmental intentions are turning against the trees we need.

Make no mistake, we need our trees more than we need most other things.

They give us the air we breathe.

It's not a spectacular forest, this forest of mine. It isn't cuddly or stunningly photogenic in the main.. It may be more like an endangered toad than the spotted owl, in terms of sexiness.

The growth is middling old to newish, depending on just where I am. The trees and plants are New Englandly. It is short some of the majestic species that once called it home.

We don't have flowers a yard wide, trees 2,500 years old or taller than mountains, grizzly bears, or forests without roads and houses. The diversity of the forest was diminished and is diminishing from a 400 - year onslaught by men and women moving west and moving in, and weeds and insects with them. Most of our animals are not endangered—yet.

But here, trees prepare for spring every fall, animals and the wind disperse seeds, salamanders hide in the litter on the forest floor for the entire winter, maples lose their leaves in a fantastic show of color, and young beeches hold onto them for most of the winter, slowly bleaching and thinning until they are as ephemeral as a breath of air as they fall into the track my skis made yesterday.

We have a real forest, and lots of it. For now. Time to get to work appreciating it.

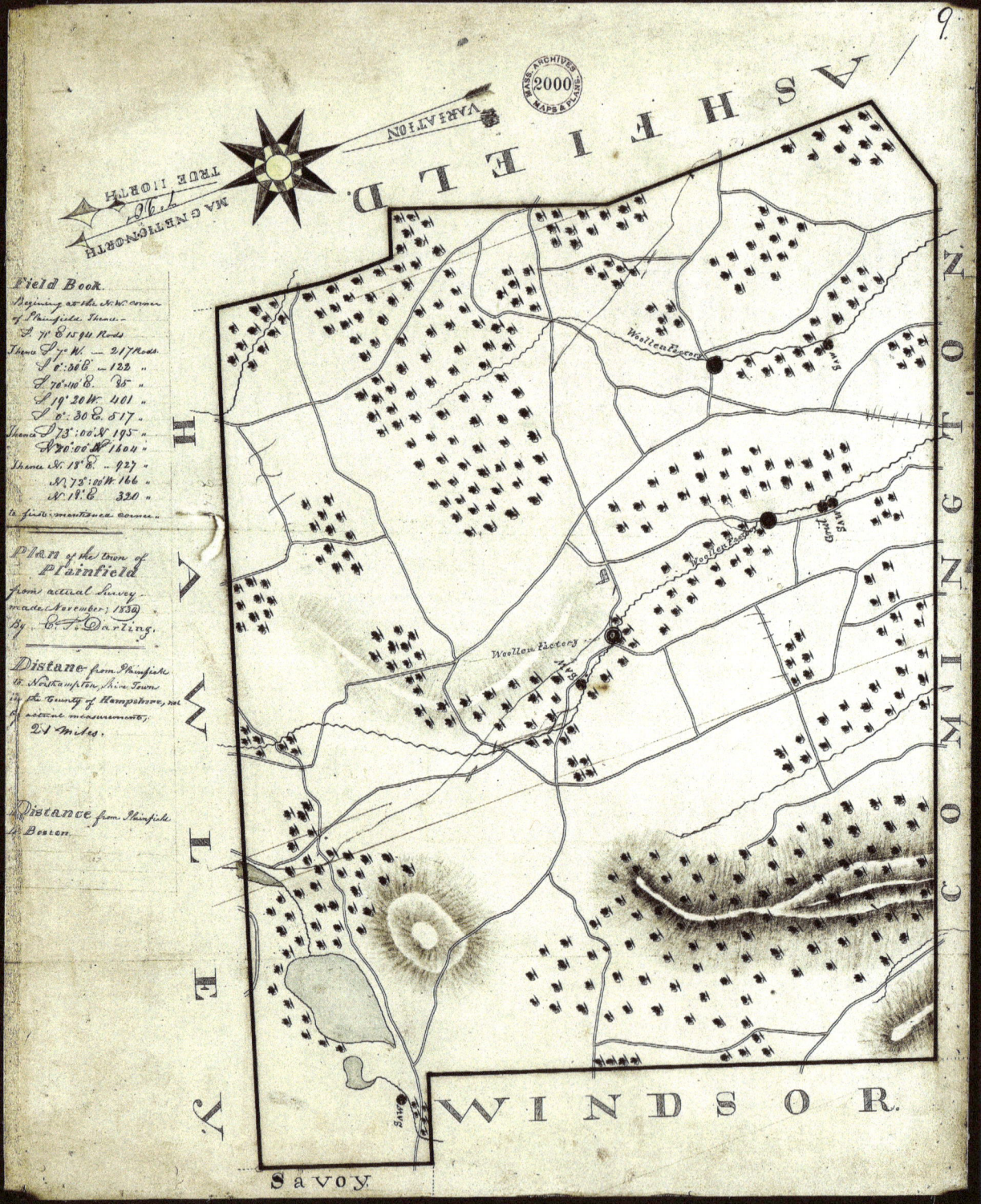

ASHFIELD

VARIATION

TRUE NORTH 7.96°
MAGNETIC NORTH

2000
MASS. ARCHIVES
MAPS & PLANS

Field Book.
Beginning at the N.W. corner
of Plainfield. Thence
S. 71° E. 154 Rods
Thence S. 19° W. — 217 Rods
S. 0°: 36 E. — 122 "
S. 76° 10' E. 85 "
S. 19° 20 W. 401 "
S. 0°: 30 E. 517 "
Thence S. 75°: 00' N. 195 "
N. 70°: 00' N. 1604 "
Thence N. 18° E. 927 "
N. 75°: 00 W. 166 "
N. 18° E. 320 "
to first mentioned corner.

Plan of the town of
Plainfield
from actual Survey
made November, 1830
By E. T. Darling.

Distance from Plainfield
to Northampton, Shire Town
in the County of Hampshire, as
of actual measurements,
21 Miles.

Distance from Plainfield
to Boston.

HAWLEY

CUMMINGTON

Woollen Factory

Woollen Factory

Saw

Woollen Factory

Saw

Saw

WINDSOR.

Savoy

Savoy

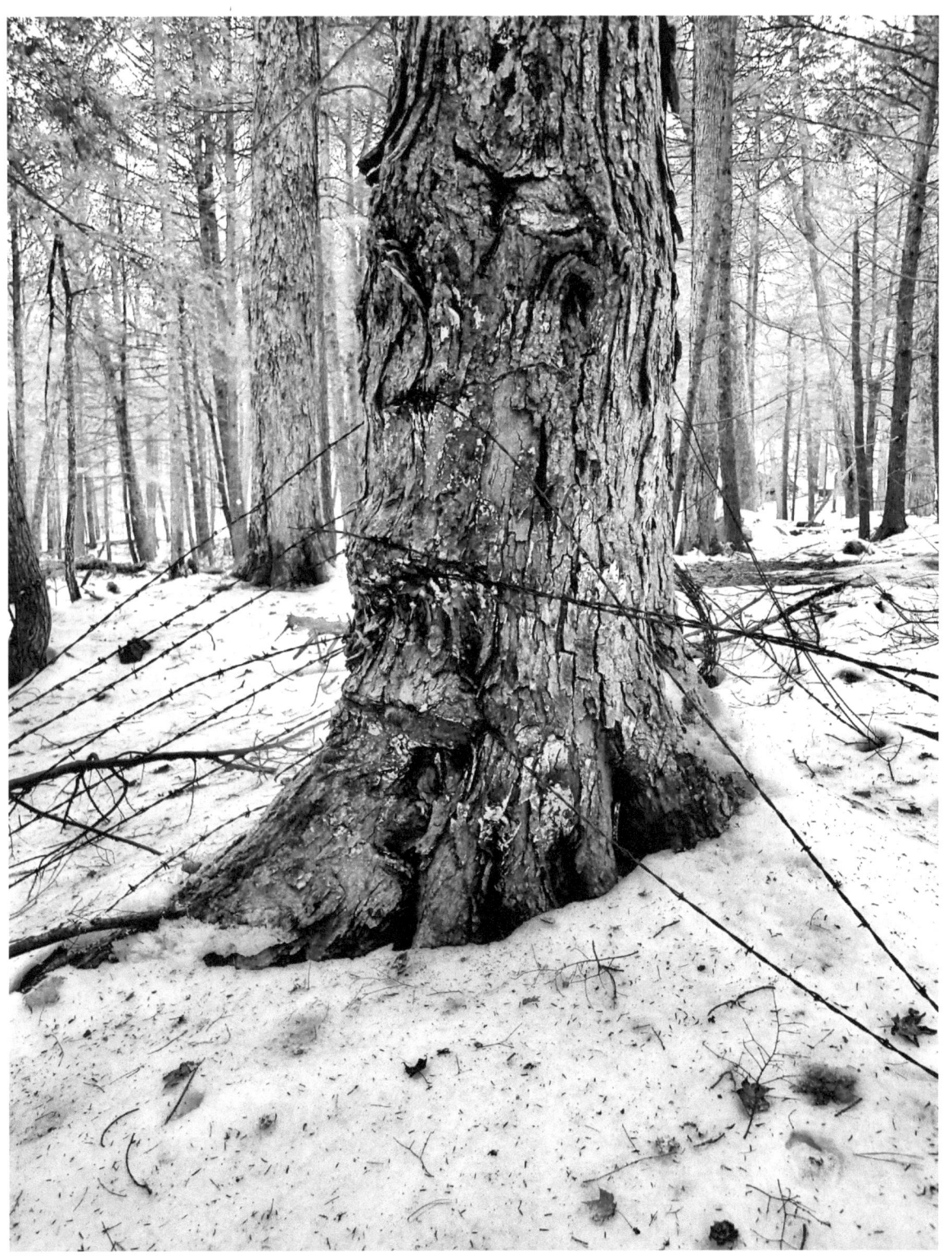

Why *Beech?*

The beech anchors the forest. Or it did, in any case.

Before settlement by people of European descent, the forest in these hills had not, like the forests on the coast, been managed. It was a mix of hardwoods, conifers, and pines.

What we see today as old-growth (or close to it) forest is dominated by hemlocks that give it its stately sense of mystery — we expect fairies and druids just around the corner. But the old old forest was dominated by towering beeches, chestnuts, elms, and some maple along with the hemlocks.

Stately, smooth-barked, giant hardwood beeches is what the potash makers were after as they speculated and slashed and burned their way through the townships Massachusetts Bay had put up for auction.*

Potash, not just used for soap, but for making glass, dyeing fabrics, and making gunpowder. Potash for export to Britain's industry. Land clearing paid for itself in potash production.

Still, they left some, and many of the old deeds of the early settlers that followed this capitalist boom delineate ownership in a world absent of human architecture by marking beech trees. Not only were they long-lived, but even after they fell groves of beeches continued to grow where the old giant once stood.

Elm and chestnut are largely gone, victims of imported blight. The beech fell victim too, but it is still here. They are everywhere, in fact. But they no longer tower. Once mature, beech bark disease gets them. I have seen many a vigorous young beech, getting ready to hit its stride, snapped in half like a match stick about halfway up its trunk. In its persistence in the face of onslaught, diminished yet pervasive, the beech embodies the spirit of the forest.

For the human, beeches still shape the experience of being in the woods, though differently. We walk among tall pines, black cherries, maple, or hemlocks as we do in a cathedral. But we are at eye level with the beeches as with the likeness of a saint in a side chapel, their leaves drawing our eye into a precisely delineated geometry of shapes, a translucent halo in the early sun of January to December.

To me, the beech is the icon of the forest.

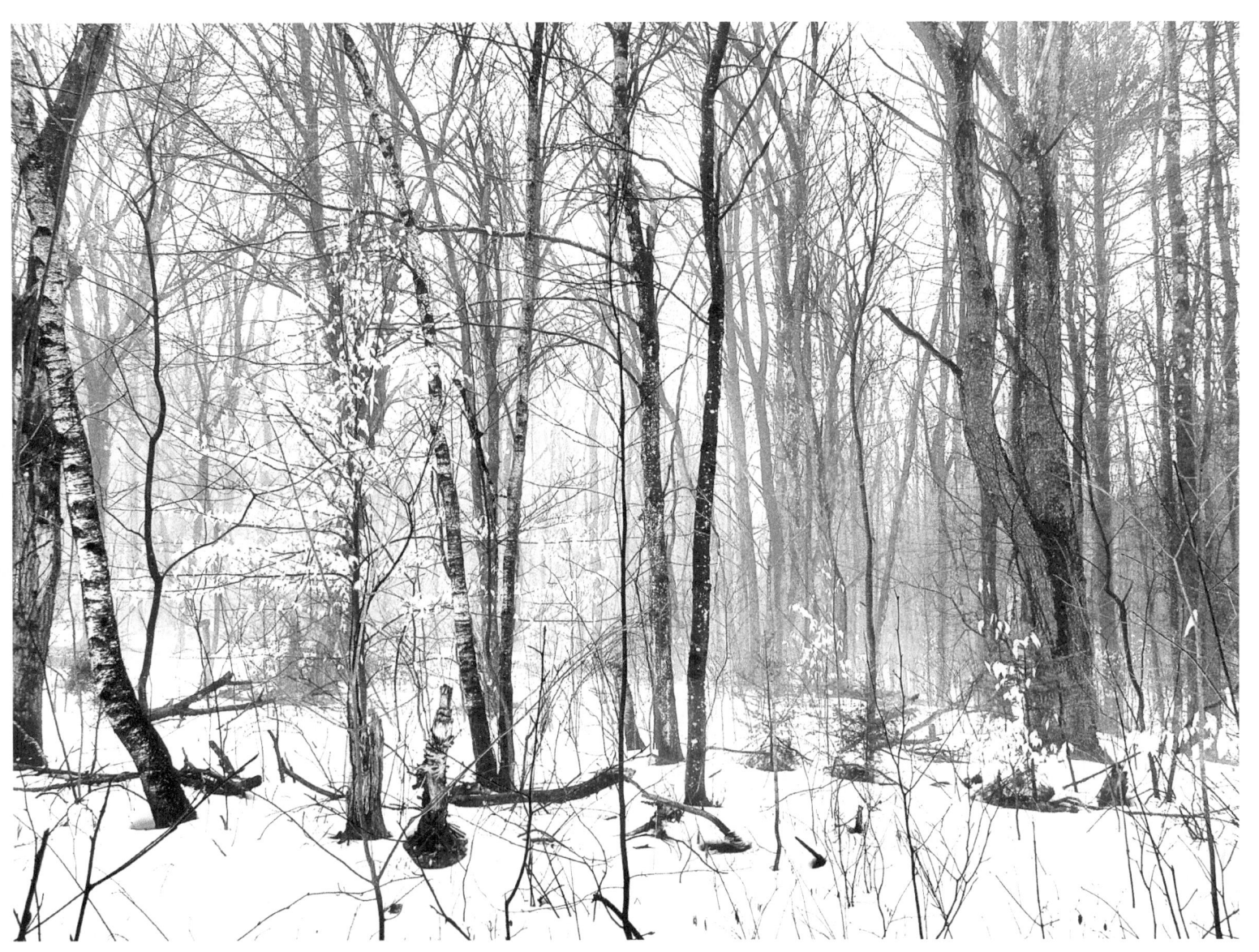

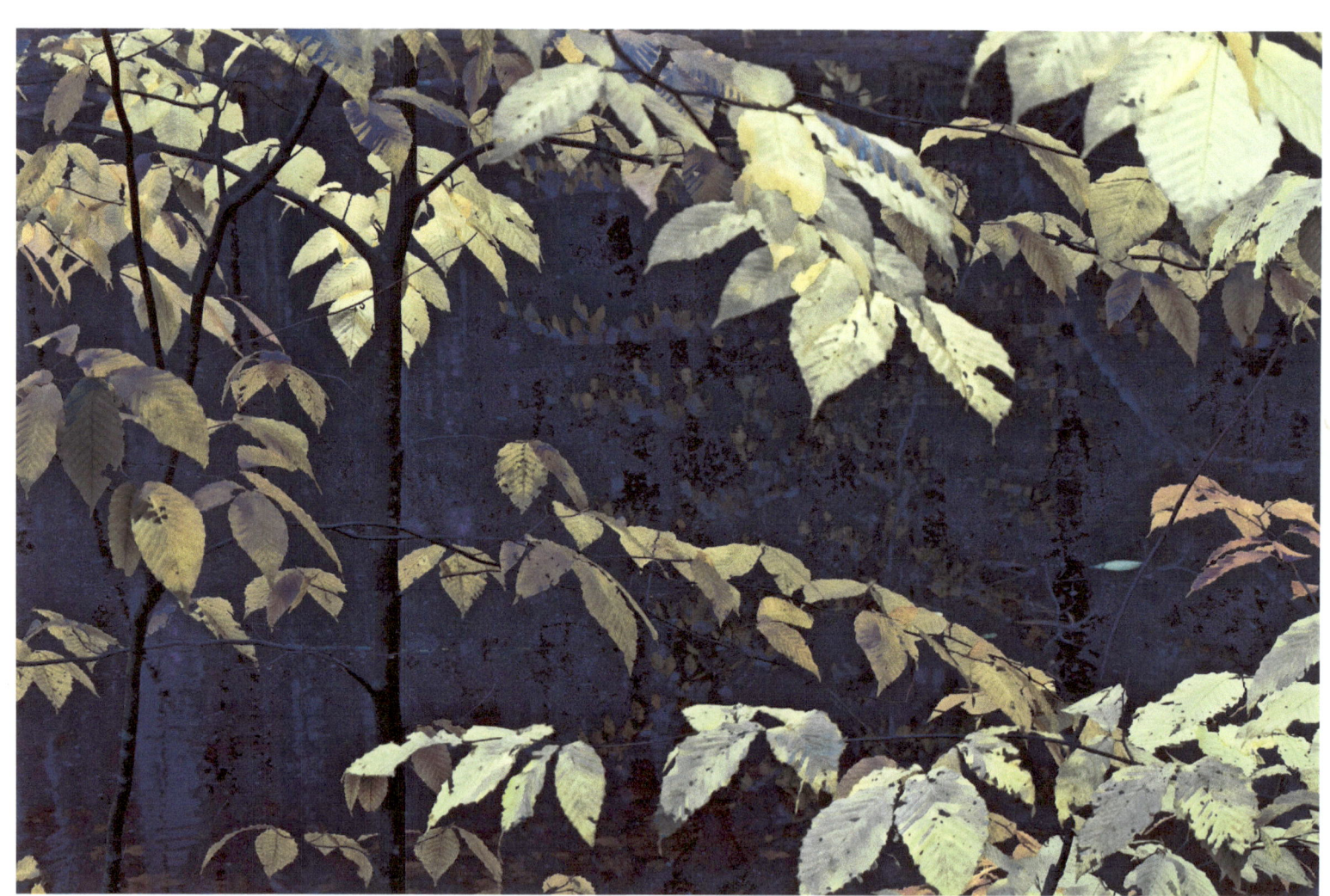

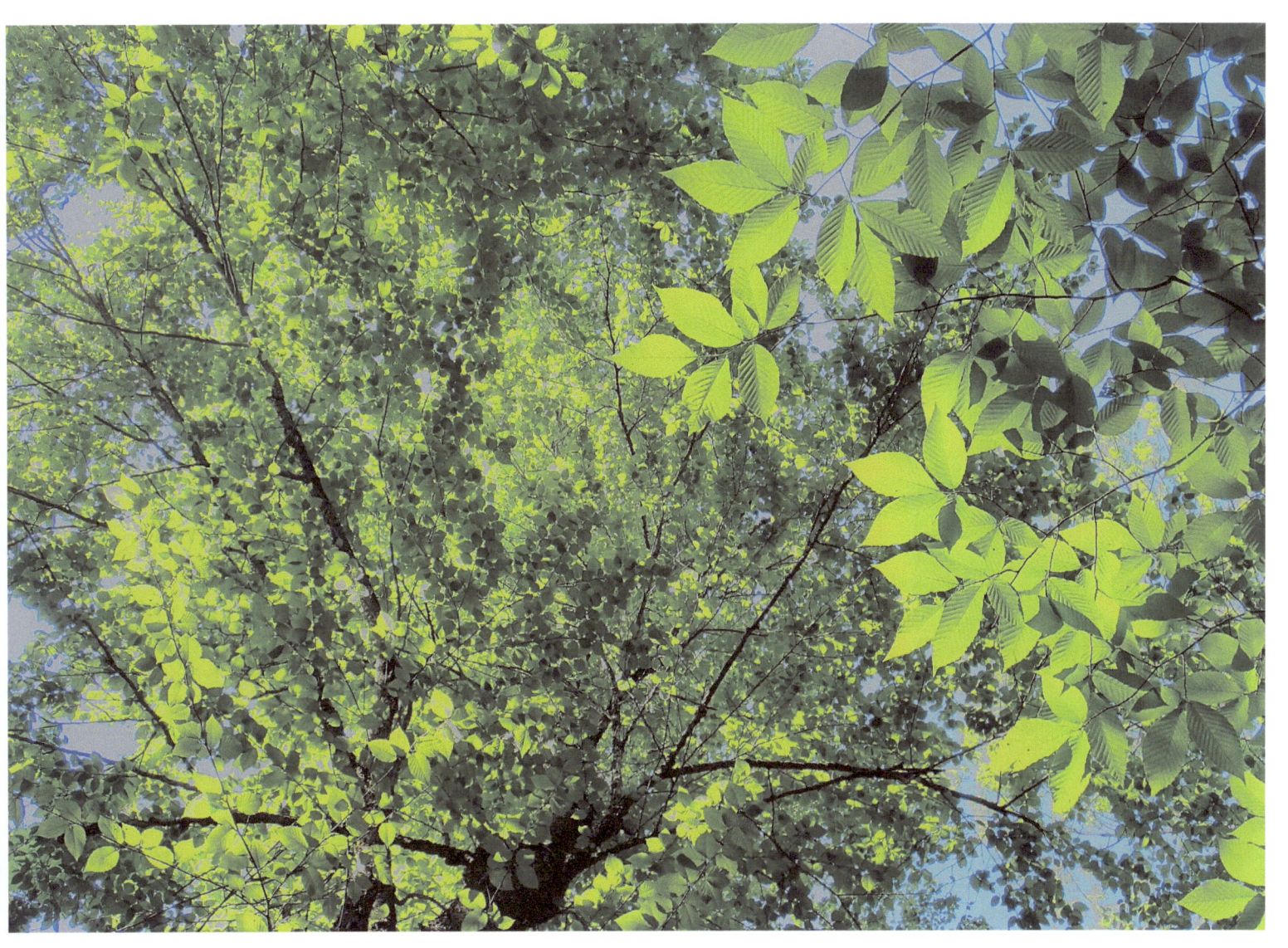

The unexpected bounty of a couple of feet of snow in March set off a frenzy of skiing.

It took me three days to break trail on the loop: up and down the old road in the woods; left on the small field on the way to the beaver pond; right by the stone wall separating the level ground from a particularly muddy perched wetland, now frozen; left through an old opening in the wall; right onto the grown-over big field, followed by hairy descent down the mowed swath, now an ice rink. Right at the bottom onto the old road; trudging up, up, and up the old road, and finally wheee! down the last hill back home.

Happy dogs. Hound and visiting half-hound jump at each other while running as fast as they can. Or simply roll around in a tussle right in front of me on the trail, particularly on steep icy sections where control is iffy in the first place. "Wheeeeee, gogogogogo!" I urge the dogs in feeble hopes that they will notice me and step aside thus avoiding a nasty spill of skis and ski poles and dogs and woman all in a pile.

When the hound is alone he loves going after my skis and poles like a pack of wolves chasing a sled in Czarist Russia, with me frantically waving my ski poles behind me so as to not have 90 pounds of hound land on the back of one of my skis mid-hill. Whew!

Despite cold and snow, the woods are in spring-wind-up. It's way below freezing but it smells damp. The schussing of my skis is accompanied by a chorus of bird song. At the least provocation prodigious melting starts with sap dripping down the outside of trees, leaving an indiscreet stain on the snow.

My trail catches beech leaves lately attached. Having stuck it out on their trees all winter, ethereal, bleached and paper thin, they show their veins and blemishes against translucent yellow. I have become obsessed with these fragile reminders of a once-mighty beech forest, each tiny veined imprint onto the universe lit as if from within, and worth a lifetime on its own account.

Photographing them is a production. Dropping poles, crouching on skis, fumbling for my glasses, trying to get the settings right, hoping the shot is in focus.

Just when I am sure I have the right exposure, focus, and enough speed to undo the wobble of crouching, a dog nose inserts itself into the scene: "hey, what are you up to? I am waiting for you!" If I'm lucky, I can press the shutter before a large paw pushes the fragile object deeply into the snow to become part of some future tree.

If I don't get up I will get nudged, and licked, and nudged until at last I give in and fall over, to be hit by a ball of tumbling dogs, playing as if our lives depended on it.

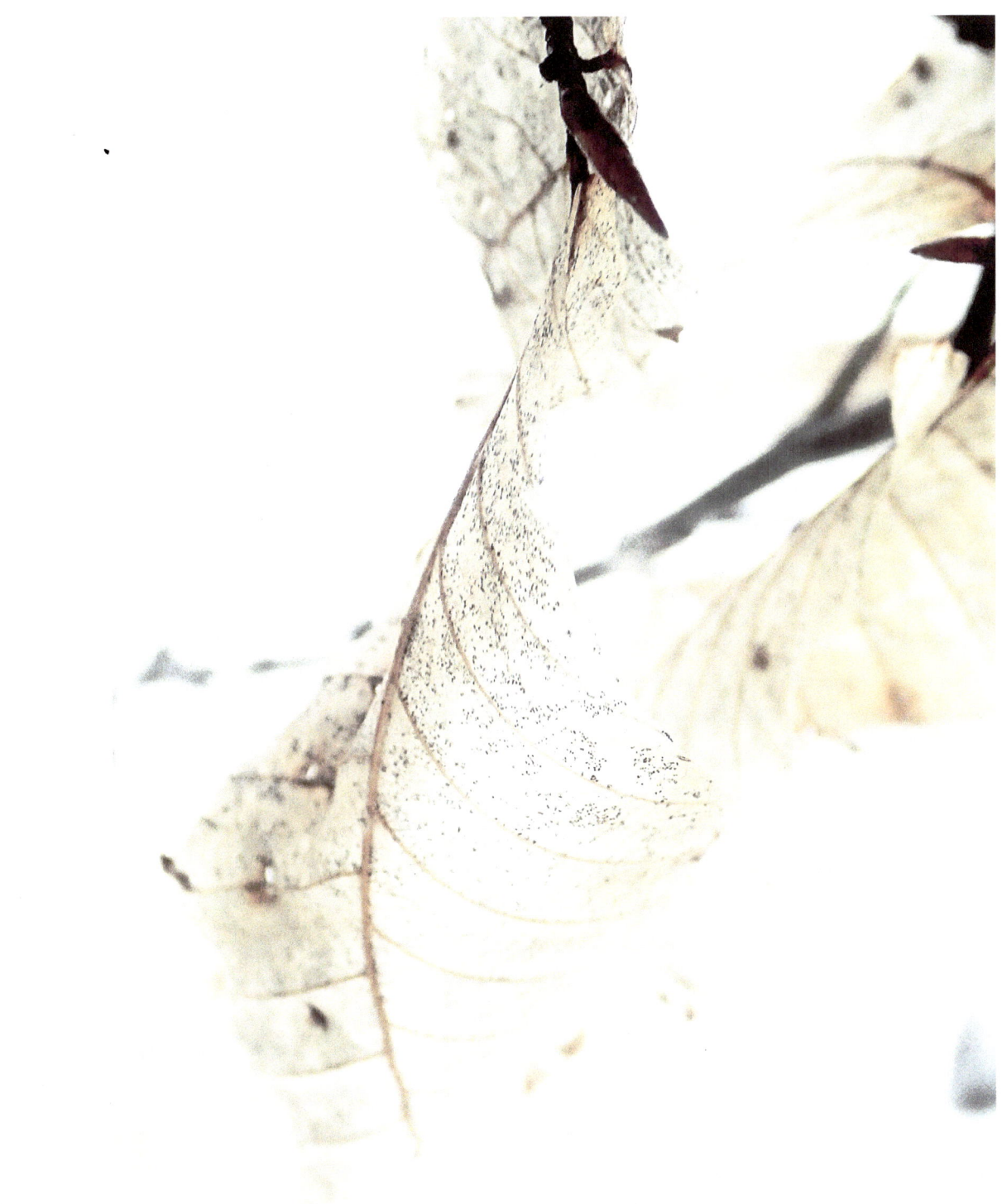

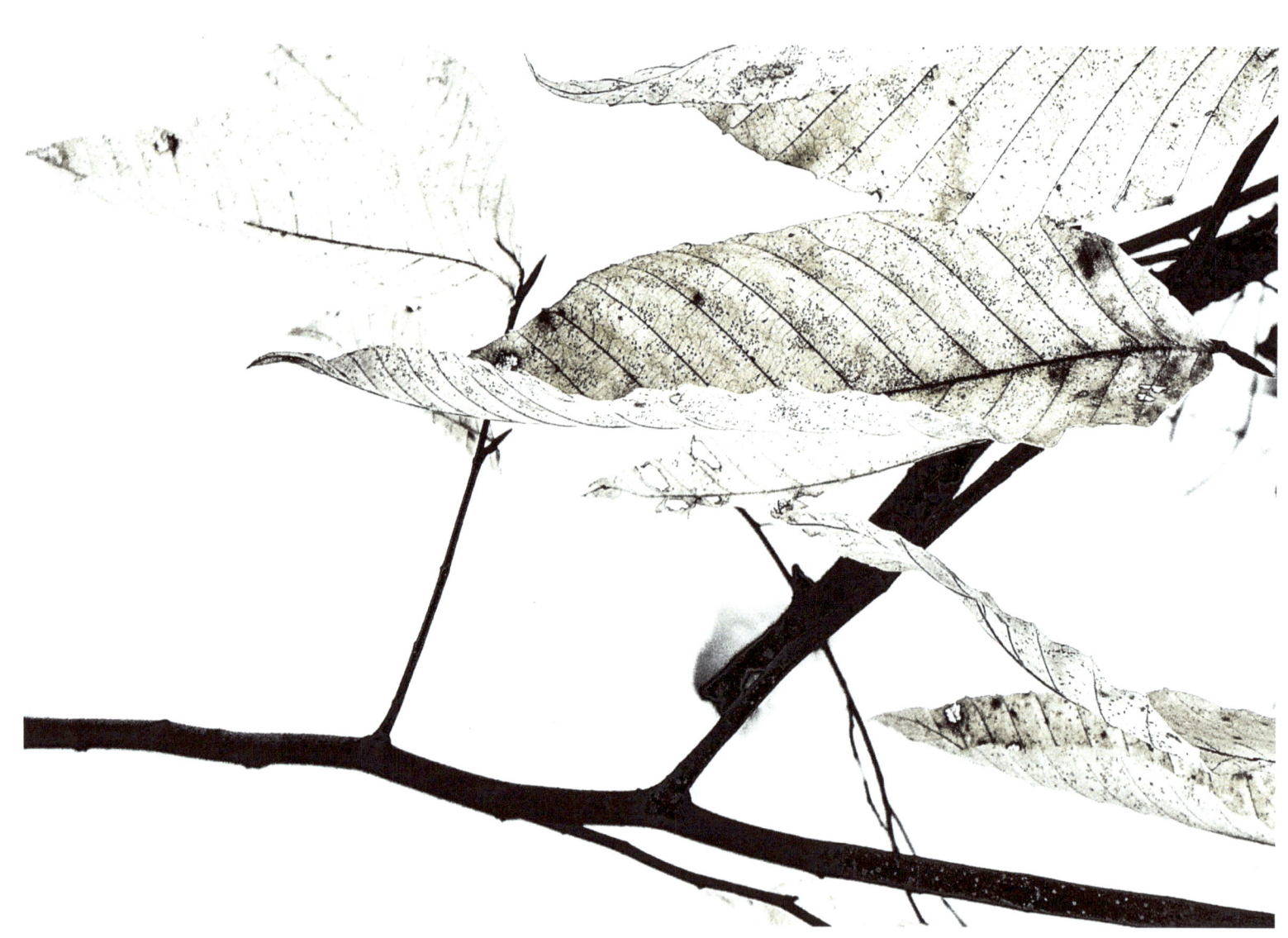

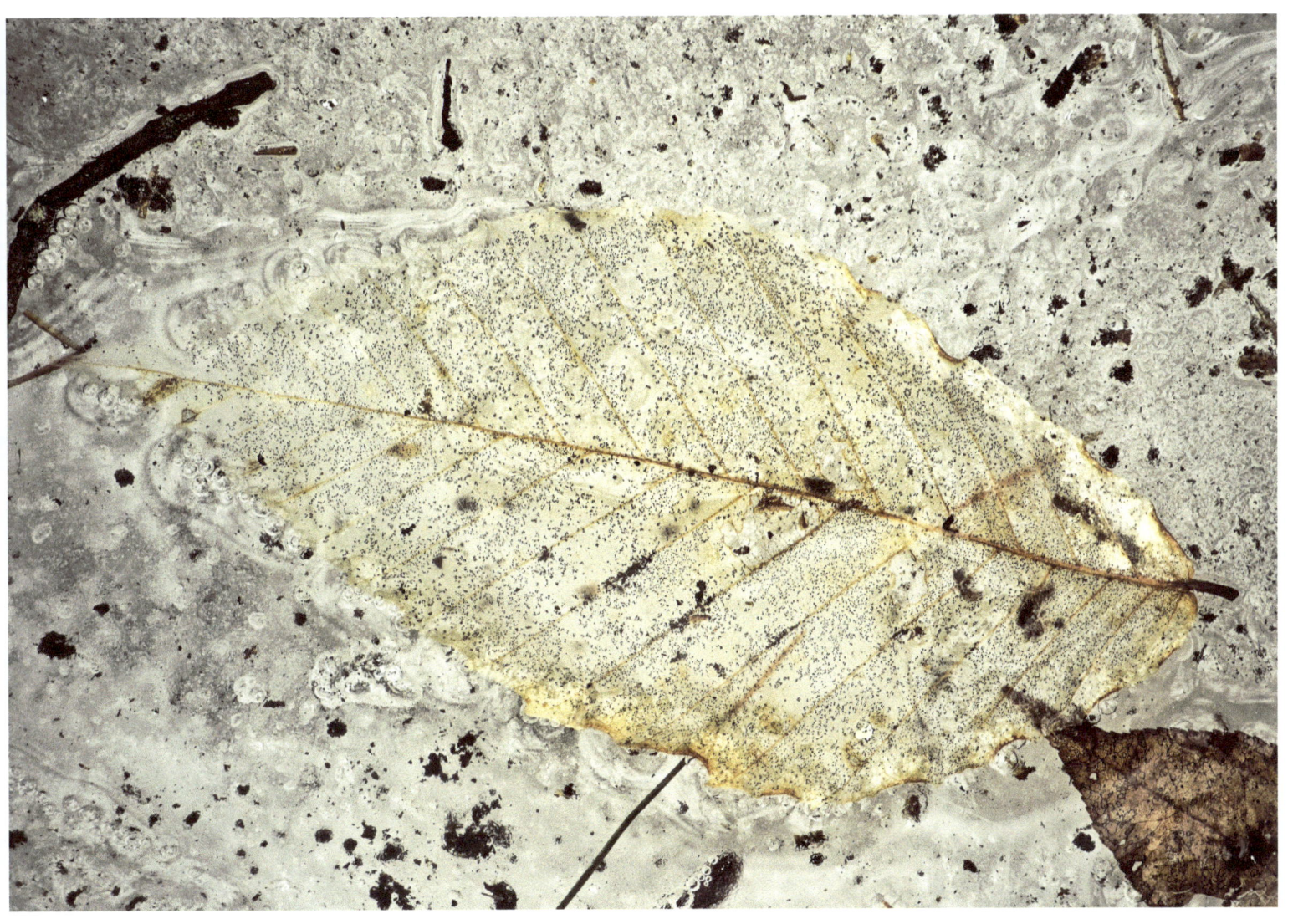

On November 29, 1811, John Packard of Plainfield sold 13 1/2 acres of land to Sarah Porter of Cummington, spinster. Roughly ten football fields in size, the land was not on a road, but marked by the corner of someone else's lot and two piles of stones with a stake stuck into them. The fourth corner was indicated by "a small beach marked."

The signatures on the deed are from a web of family ties between Packards and Porters. All evidence suggests that Sarah was recently born and the recipient of a piece of her mother's inheritance, set off from the corner of one of her relatives' holdings, perhaps for her to enjoy when she herself got married. Every expectation was that Plainfield would not remain a small backwater for long. The deed was recorded years later in Northampton, on April 16, 1824.

All of this is conjecture based on fragile evidence. The reality is likely to have been completely different. Other than on this deed, Sarah's name is nowhere to be found. But everyone else shows up in the record, suggesting a complex web of exchanges that resulted in this and maybe also other deeds. They were indelible exchanges on paper and in memory. But on the ground they were marked by less permanent signs, like stone walls, piles of stones, and carvings in beech trees.

The exact location of Sarah's piece of land is lost in the mist of time. Since beech trees don't heal their bark and grow old and tall, the small beech tree would have been expected to carry Sarah's markings that her marriage, and much beyond that perhaps, to take care of her needs in old age.

Carved in beech, it was anything but written in stone, of course, and contemporary deeds show that reliance was on memory as much as physical signs. On September 14, 1830, William Pratt sold or mortgaged two pieces of land to Amos Tirrell, his neighbor. The first is described as "being the the land deeded by Daniel L. Pratt to the said Wm. Pratt."

The western edge of the other was on a road and obvious, but its eastern boundary ran along a pretty iffy line, designated by a stake and stones in the "original boundary line" of a larger lot, then in a south-westerly direction to a maple stump with a stake in it, and then "about the same course to a beech tree marked on two sides."

Even as memory and tradition may have served amiably at the time, on the ground, without reference to exact points, without GPS, and with few roads, things were not quite as orderly as the myriad recorded transactions seem to suggest. The picture that emerges to me is of roughly cleared land with a few roads and stone walls but not that many yet, some piles of stones and stumps with (metal? wood?) stakes stuck in them, and, here and there, parcels with trees including beeches which are recognized by all and handy for marking where you are.

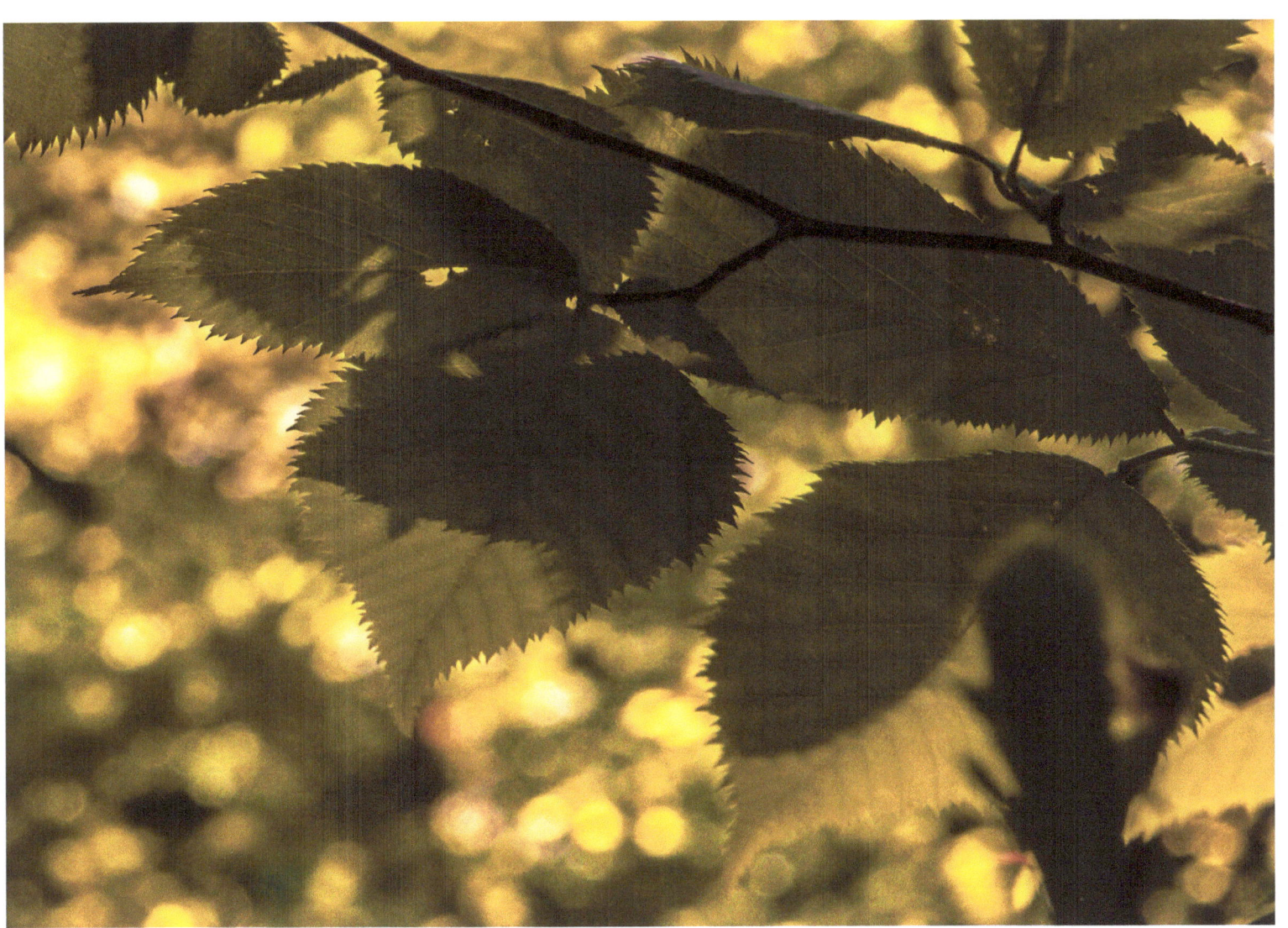

There's an orderly and proper sequence for winter and spring. It lives in my head and your head and seemingly nowhere else. But we profit in camaraderie from sharing the knowledge.

Yesterday we trudged up the hill across the street to a place called the Pinnacle on a map made for this land … three ski resorts and two institutions for the unadjusted ago. The going was tough, with about eight inches of ice snowy stuff that made it like trudging on the beach but then up the hill.

Along the way are vernal pools and stinky marshy areas that in the summer the hound will sniff with abandon and stay out of sight coming back black and muddy and with a grin on his face after we've gone worried.

But we're not there yet and we thought about how it might be that a few weeks from now the frogs will have made their music and laid their eggs in these pools now filled with ice having gone greenish and brownish with the rain that fell over the last week mingled with the pool itself melting and then freezing.

We were remarking and agreeing that it looked like early March.

But it didn't really because every winter season has its own bent, much in the way that the summer brings a proliferation of different creatures each year. One year you notice it's naught but forget-me-nots out there, even in places where you'd never known them to grow before. The next you're obsessively crawling on your belly through sopping grass at dawn and dusk to catch the sun lighting up dandelion fluff just so because the dandelions have the world.

And then the third year is a bit unfortunate and cause of much complaining because rats have taken advantage of a warm winter and extra seed and few owls or whatever else it is that makes them proliferate, you see them everywhere and you have to fight them off at every possible gap in the 200-year old hole in the ground lined with fieldstone that you call your basement.

Nature just won't behave in a quiet and orderly fashion, and we always complain that we never get the amount of Spring we're supposed to get in our own sense of what is due us. How could we.

—

This year's slow onset of spring has its own rewards. All has been browns and grays. Paper-thin beech leaves dressing up the woods until green starts to emerge. Little tinklers and waters rushing through sand and rocks and dead leaves. Springs popping up left and right. Bogs and pools lying back, waffling leisurely and endlessly between ice and water. Two wet feet every day from intimate scrutiny.

Our two days of spring are here. By this afternoon, green and red will take the palette for the season. Let the riot commence.

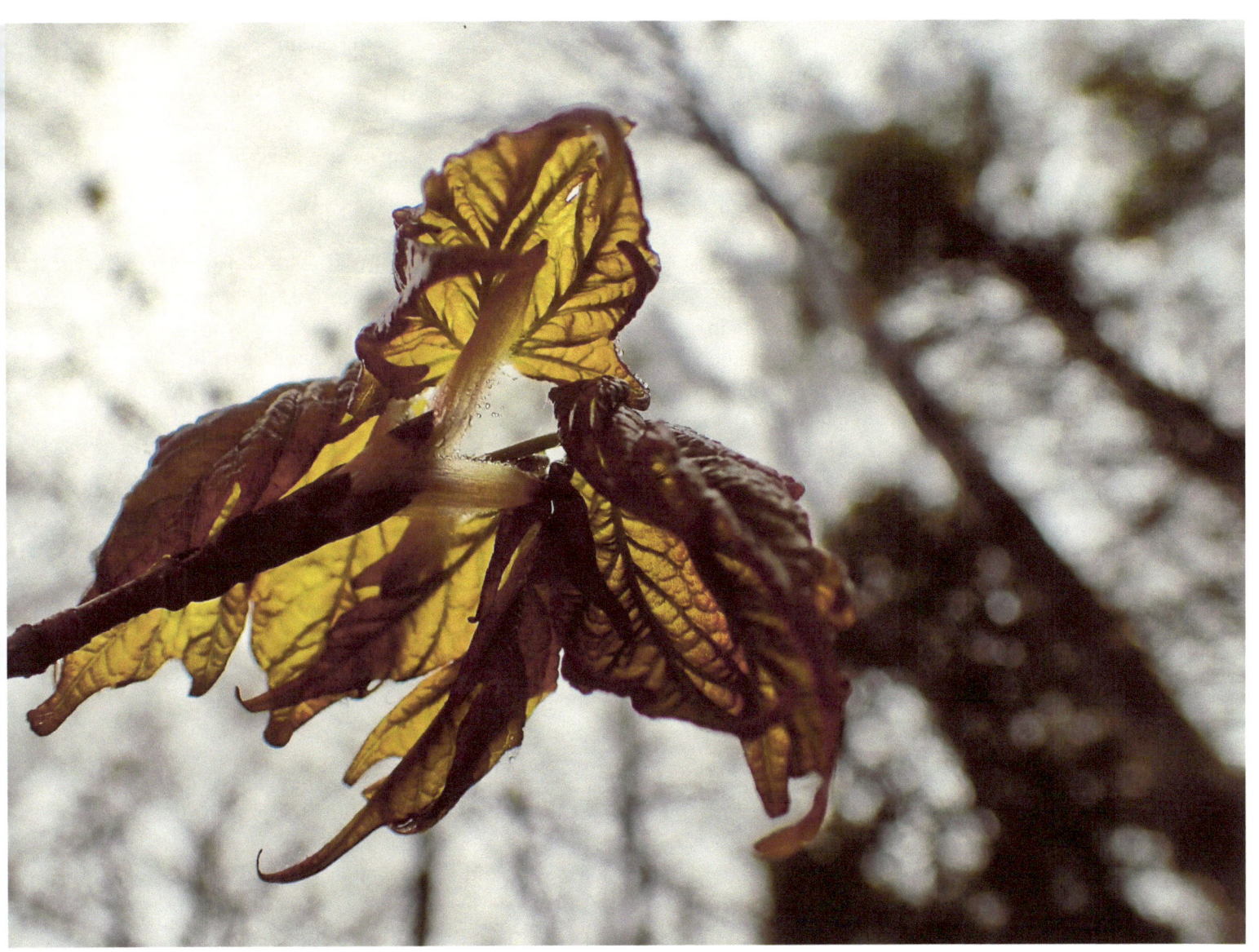

The other day I looked at a blog called *nature has no boss* that is inspired by "that which happens of its own accord" and I have been talking back to it ever since.

Unfortunately it looks like earth's nature does have a boss in the long run, and we're about to decisively win the race.

On the other hand, experiencing nature moves us, or many of us at least, like nothing else despite our complicity in taking it down. There are some I know who don't give a shit, or who do care in the abstract but personally could not care less. In the main, they are few.

Most of us simply suffer from a lack of patience to slow down and pay attention — or perhaps it is a lack of habit. We need a kick in the butt like a blizzard to notice nature that happens. And even then…

But 'that which happens of its own accord' is going at it in full force around us all the time even when it's not earth-shattering or caused by climate change. Physics and biology don't pay attention to what we think is major.

Today, my footsteps tinkle small alerts as I crunch along, stomping hard to put my feet and the ice under them on notice that I am not planning on going down this hill ass over teakettle. Staking out my ground.

Ice just is, but it will take apart mountains by becoming again and again and again. The grasses in the bog are caught in ice and snow, they just have to sit there and take it. No stomping the feet.

Up the hill, tall trees are swaying and creaking ominously in the polar wind like the grand staircase in an abandoned mansion when the bad guy is creeping up with murder on his mind.

They stand there, summer and winter, all their lives, being part of that which happens of its own accord and taking it as it comes: heat, cold, drought and the 11 inches in one day of hurricane Irene.

When it gets to be too long or just too soggy for their equilibrium they fall over and it's done. And of their own accord they rot. That, too, is awesome to witness if you take a moment to look.

It happens to people all the time, this of its own accord business, but in our altered human reality we don't like it and don't believe it. Mothers and prayers tell us to accept that which we cannot change, but we are hardwired to fight the very notion and all of its instances.

And here in the doubly altered reality that is the United States we believe that if something happens you must not have been praying or counting crystals or treading the elliptical machine assiduously enough.

"I'd strike the sun if it insulted me," cried Ahab, in response to the charge that he was blasphemous in his wish to take revenge on nature by killing the white whale that maimed him. (*Moby Dick*, Chapter 36)

Deep down inside we cannot believe that the system we call nature doesn't care whether we or the tree live or die, be whole or broken, that it just is.

Neither do we want to admit even to ourselves that we have created our own systems in the image of the white whale or the storm, instead of that of the merciful father and promise of heaven or the orderly world in which effort brings rewards that we think we believe in.

We encounter the homeless man on the street and hold tight to the small splinter of hope that he must have done something wrong — lest we are next, smote down by Ahab's harpoon.

The trees just are and the ice just is. But if I can pay enough attention, stop just a moment to hijack the sun as it climbs slowly into and above the trees and sends a tendril of light in my direction across icy snow, I can see how gorgeously it is, happening of its own accord.

And how it is so much bigger than I am.

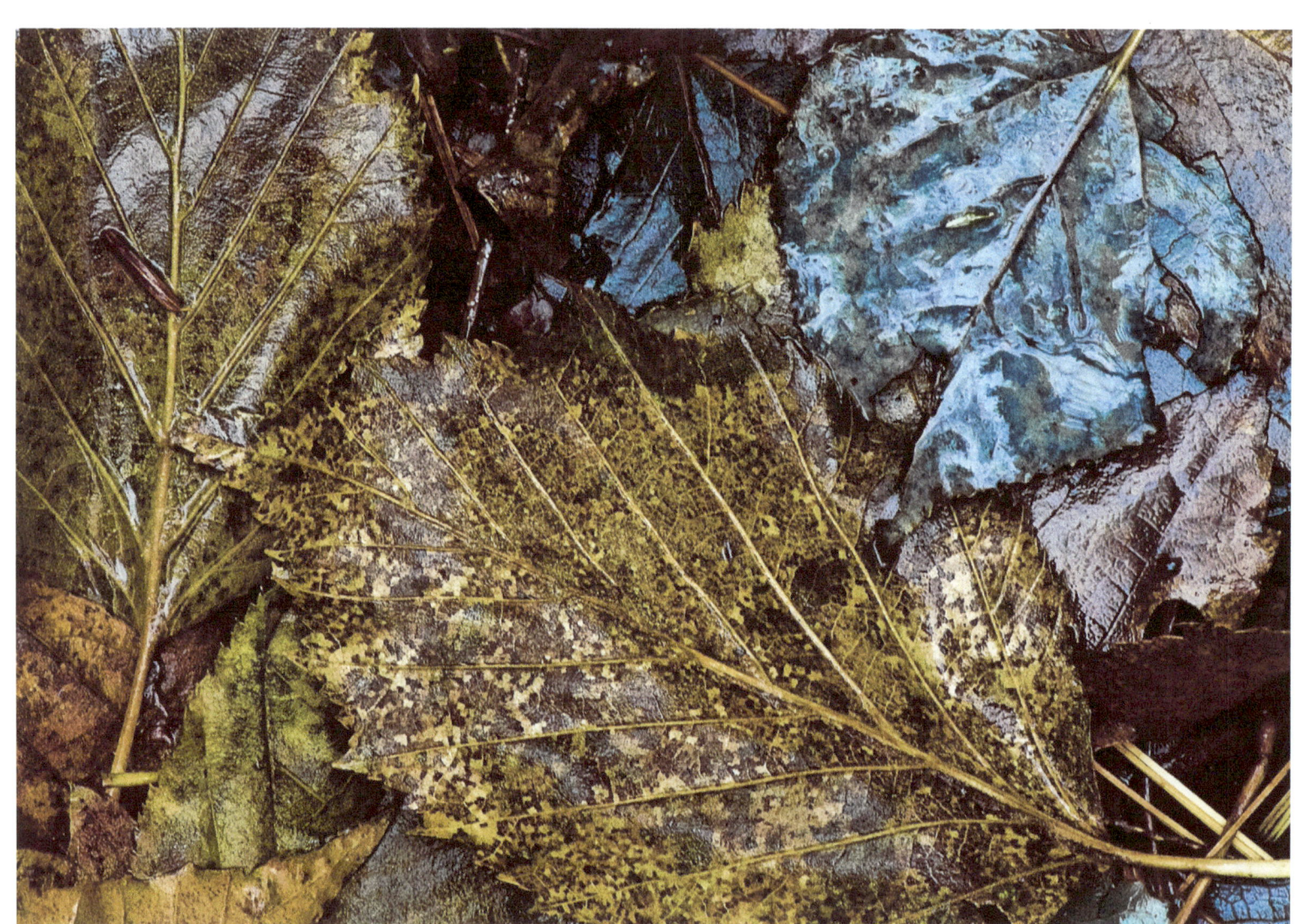

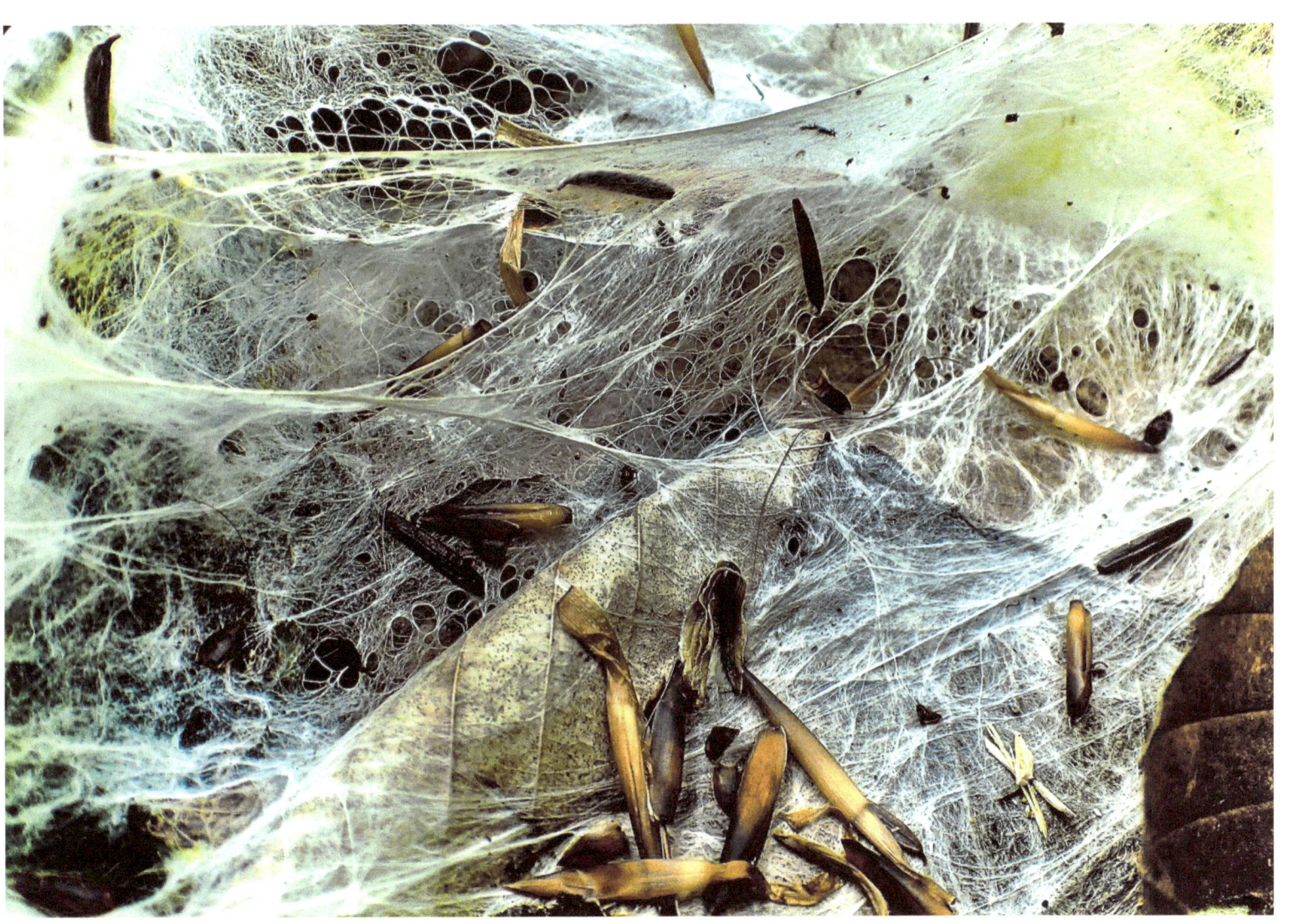

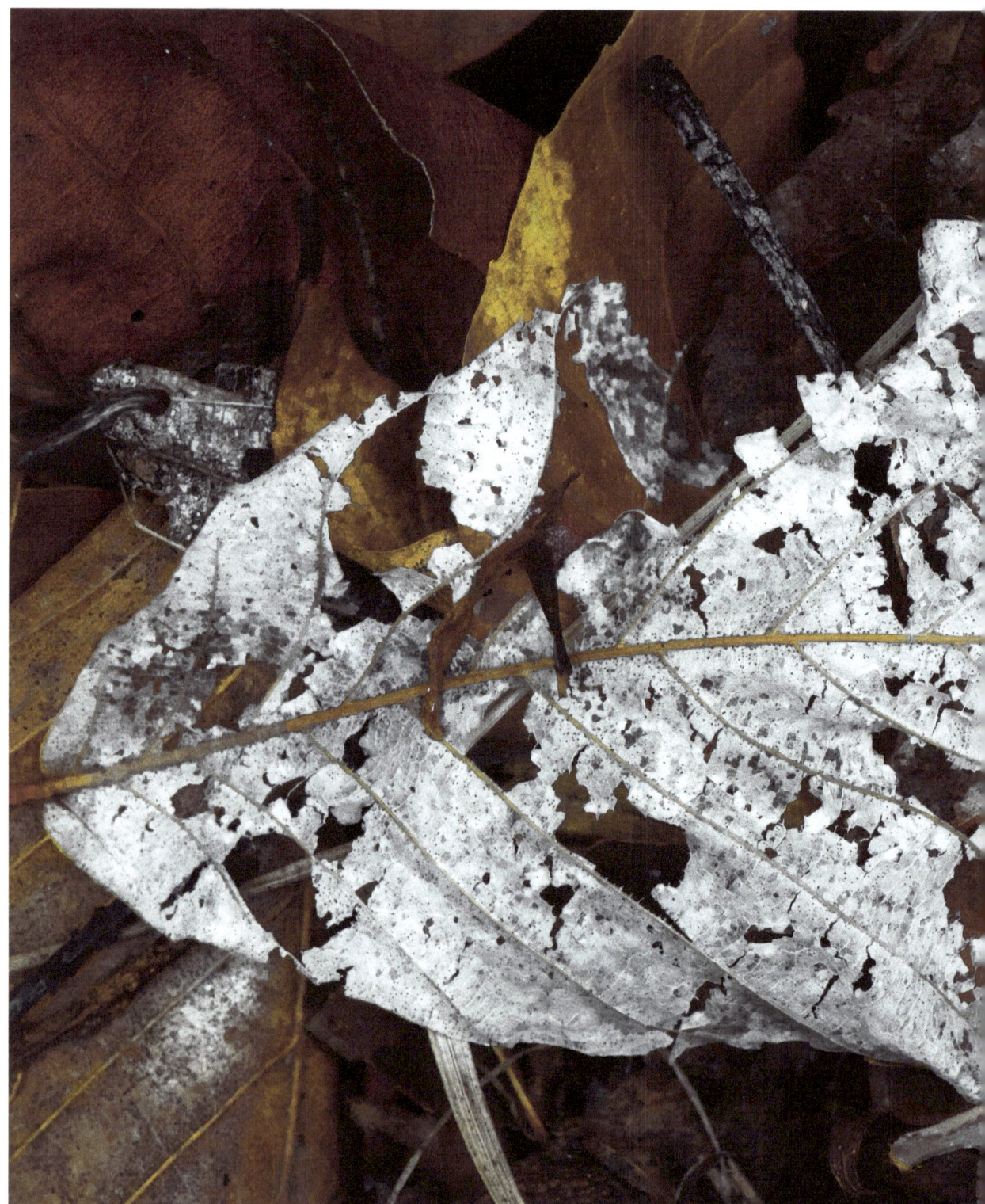

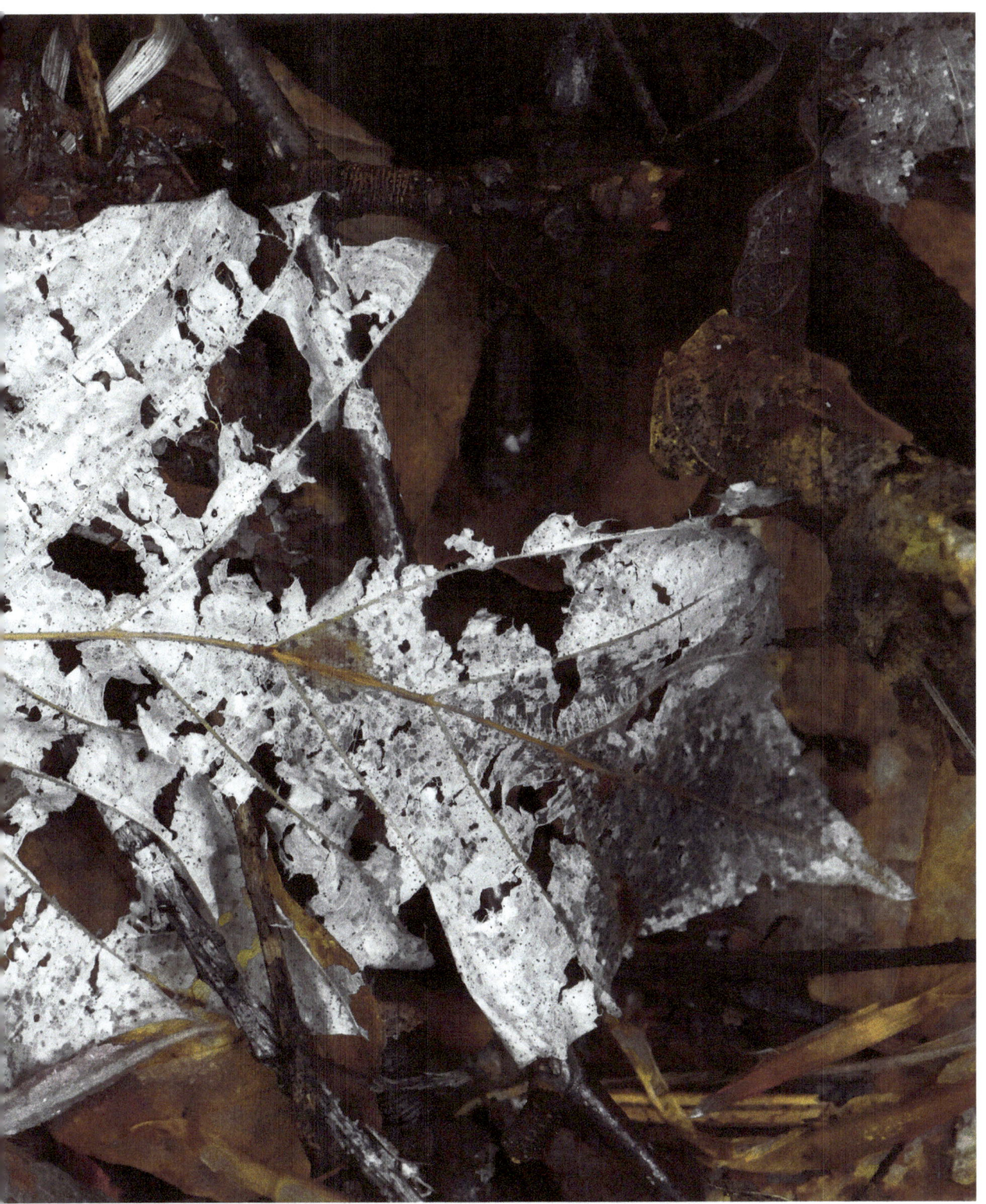

When you hang out with naturalists too much you get inducted into a society of words that sound ordinary but are precise scientific terms.

Consider *vernal pool* — a pond that exists in the spring and dries up the rest of the year through a process they (the naturalists) call *evapotranspiration*. We know what that is, we do it ourselves. Apparently the vernal pool hails from California where they transpire in the spring and are empty the rest of the year, and ours aren't the real thing because we have the wrong climate so they are often also filled in the fall. But they use the term here nonetheless.

Plus ours, at least in Plainfield, take place in the woods — that's what we have, mostly. Important because all sorts of amphibians lay their eggs in them.

The vernal pool has *obligate species* and *indicator species*. The former species breed in vernal pools 99% of the time. They need the vernal pool to breed in. The latter are the same but seen from the pool's point of view. These species, when present. tell you this pool is the real thing.

To sum it up, a vernal pool is a temporary but cyclically occurring piece of water on which certain species depend entirely for their existence. Wood frog and fairy shrimp being two of them. No vernal pool, no species. That is kind of a scary thing if you think of it.

Plainfield is rife with vernal pools. What makes them so likely here is that right under the soil we have rocky ledge or glacial till (which is like concrete, but made by glaciers instead of in factories. Unlike concrete, it is not one of the leading single causes of global warming). In other words, we have some soil, but don't need to go far down until, clink, you hit a layer that water won't go through.

Or your shovel for that mater. I can assure you that digging 4-foot holes for footings when the till is at 2 ain't for sissies such as myself. In any case, the water likes to lie on top of that layer when there's a bit of a depression. Add a more or less continuous supply of water and you have a *perched wetland*, which has its own obligate species I am sure, but that's a different story.

If your water supply is only available as a result of spring runoff and high ground water levels, and it dries up but not too fast under the trees you may have a certifiable vernal pool (yes Virginia, vernal pools get to have certificates) if you send the right photos with the right arrows to the right people. Certified = protected by the Wetlands Protection Act. Let's get going already on certifying.…

Which is why I am witnessing a drama unfolding. Last week I was poking about some springs with my friend the stream-hopper and we found a depression caused by an infernal machine that had been poking around to see about cutting down many trees and installing a pipeline.

In it, masses of frog eggs tied underwater to sticks and stones by mama frog so they would not pop up out of the water too early. Gelatinous masses with dotted with dark heart op-art so far not having grown the tail of the tadpole. But even without the tails, I knew them as my pals to follow in their development.

I returned this weekend to see how they were doing and found the pool dried up entirely. No sign of frog eggs. I guess I just have to accept that nature makes redundancies so that even as some vernal pools dry up frogs make it in others.

Except these frogs were fooled by a pool that shouldn't have been there in the first place, a temporary aberration caused by a careless machine with no impermeable layer of glacial till or forest cover to prevent it from drying up. Multiply by 100 or 1000 and you get the drama.

But I was hooked on frogs now so I went to see the vernal pool behind the house of another friend who is a naturalist and who has not just frog eggs but also spotted salamander spermatophores. (That's' the model where dad leaves the sperm behind tacked loosely to leaves on the bottom so it won't float off, and mom comes by to pick it up. Drive-in-fertilization as it were.) Little fuzz men and less defined than the frog eggs, I've been trying to photograph them but they aren't as happy to sit for portraits.

It still hasn't rained a whole lot and today I went back to this vernal pool to see how we were doing on tadpole development only to find that it has shrunk considerably and some of the sticks with egg masses were sticking up out of the water. No rain in sight. I have a call into my pal to get him to don big boots and move the sticks into deeper water for mama frog. Not that I am a sentimentalist or anything like that.

The thing that keeps sticking in my mind is that this is such an amazing system: drive-by fertilization and temporary nurseries where the young-uns can't get too used to staying home because they dry up. Such a tricky balance with water in and water out.

Not too many vernal pools left in California I gather. I hope we do better in the long term but here, too, the bulldozer eats 40 acres a day in Massachusetts.

The whole story begs a question of course: of what are humans the *obligate* and of what are they the *indicator* species? Do we obligate aught other than destruction?

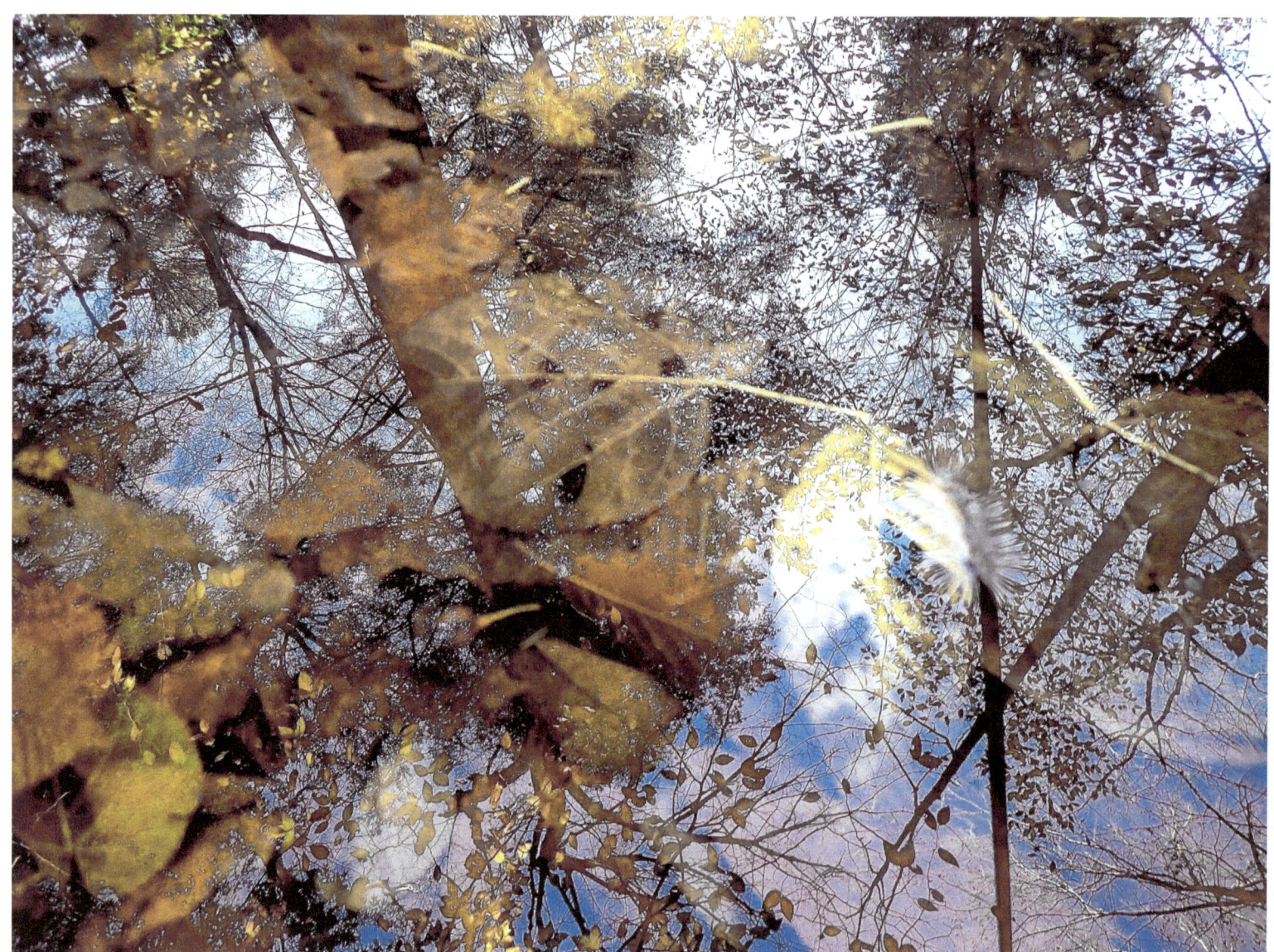

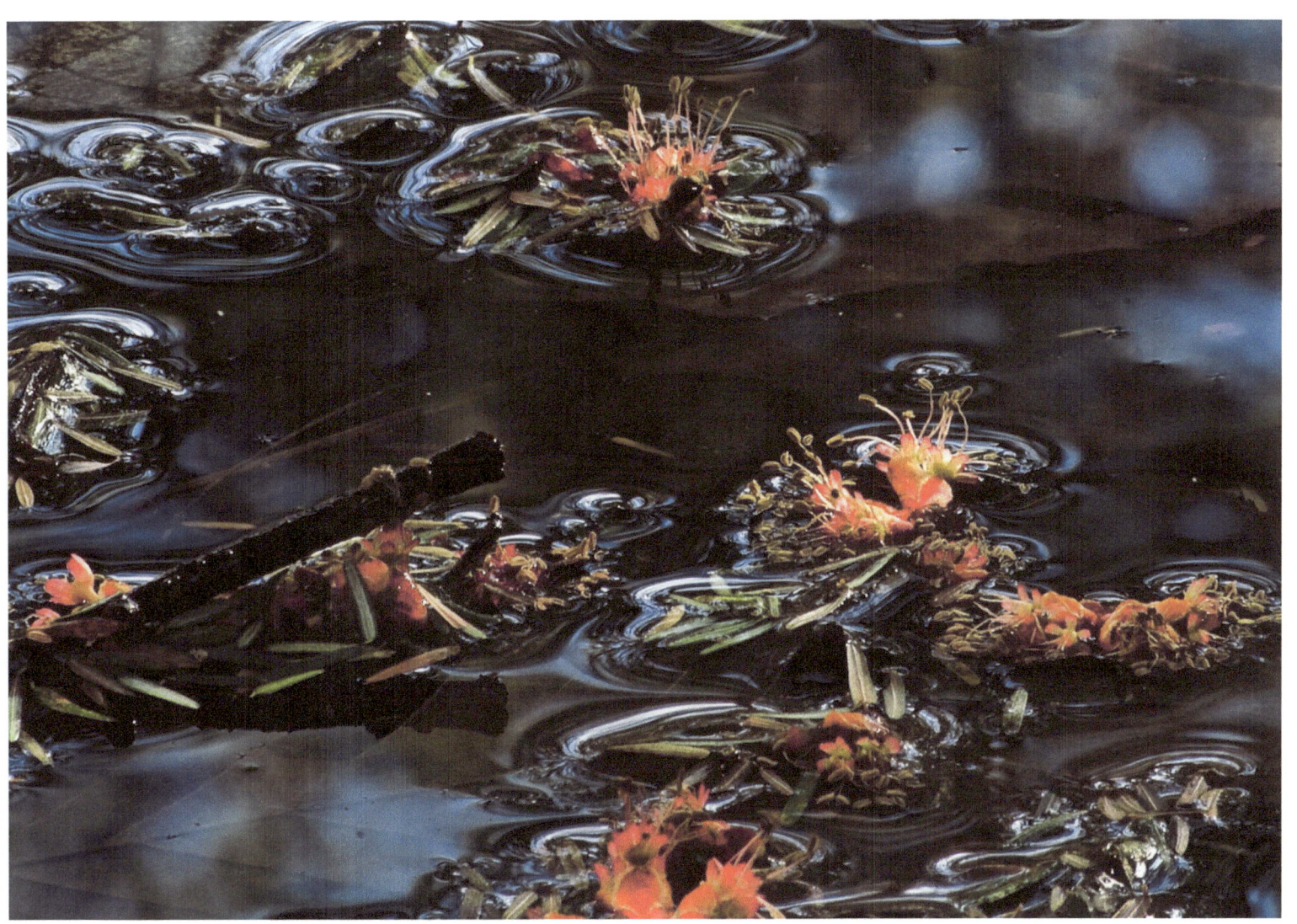

Detritus is at the center of everything, some think. A vernal pool, for instance, is characterized by having detritus as its main source of food (energy). That is, dead stuff from plants and animals not living in it. A vernal pool does not have plants or fish that die and decompose in the water. Stuff falls in and floats in on the wind. Around here, that means beech and maple leaves galore.

The pool is full of tiny chompers and cutters, creatures specialized in breaking down the leaves, twigs, pollen, dead insects, dead animals, what have you that fall into it. Kind of like a giant digestive trap. As the die, they in turn become part of the energy that get digested by even tinier creatures that eat dead things, and of course tall of them are also eaten by larger creatures. Tadpoles for instance. And then it dries up.

I learned all that during an interesting conversation with a real-life ecologist about the definition of external detritus (doesn't grow in the wet place) versus the food chain in a bog (really a marsh) where everything and everybody is part of the feast, as plants grow with the nutrients at the very base of it.

For instance, we wondered whether, if a beech tree whose roots are below the vernal pool drops its leaves into the water, it is in fact a member of the vernal pool system, even though biologists don't see that in the same way. To them, the vernal pool sort of ends at water's end, as it were, even the bottom.

The biologist also told me that when ecology started, it was assumed that each system was defined by creatures at the top of the chain, the predators we see in the pages of *National Geographic* and in scary movies. "Now we know," he said, "that it's all about like the tiny ones in the water I just showed you in the petrie dish." Donning hip waders, he'd ventured into a vernal pool to get us some stuff to look at, including the tiniest and cutest tadpoles, giving me a serious case of wader-envy in the process.

For me, it was one of those moments when you see more clearly. We create our world in the image of our own mind, and when we change that mind about ourselves, we create new scientific understanding as well and vice versa. When scientists assumed that we were at the center of everything, they saw those who are most like us in size and activities, likely meat-eating mammals, as the center of an ecosystem.

But slowly an understanding emerged that the systems are not dependent on those at the top, and many, including many scientists, began to see humans as an interdependent piece of nature, as a predator that should not overplay its hand for fear of ending up without and starving.

Much of the current political distrust of science seems to stem exactly from that moment when religion, which puts humans central in creation, became at odds with biology, in which the balance in natural systems became a central tenet.

Science isn't infallible. You have to believe in its system, the scientific method of empiricism: you have to prove your theories in practice, and you can only prove them until they are disproven. Denying that leaves you open to charges of disingenuousness.

What sets science apart from religion is that it is aware of its own fallibility. Or in any case it should be. Most scientists I have met, and some of my best friends are scientists, have a general sense of the superiority of their way of seeing things and a specific sense of their own superiority in the food chain of knowledge. But probed more seriously, they will always tell you that it holds only until the next thing comes around.

Which is not the case with popular representation of the state of scientific inquiry, which only talks of proof and truth. But we historians know that, for instance, the world of biology was greatly upset by the idea that the mammalian (including human) embryo was not, as had been assumed since Aristotle, male in creation, becoming female only by failing to remain male -- but rather more the other way around. It took some serious doing and some generations to change that assumption. That scientists, too, can be blind to the obvious or fall in love with their own beliefs, and how that fits into the scientific method as a source of "truth" about the world, is a conversation we need to have.

But I digress. Detritus — garbage as the the source of it all — it's all in a name or an assumption of value. We, and in this case that's all of us, you and me, need to stop seeing the world in our own image, creating the larger picture out of of what we can see and comprehend with our senses pleasingly — as we are busily cleaning up all the detritus around the edges of nature — replacing it with useless detritus not so distinguishable by the chompers and cutters. And remarkably barren of amino acids and the other building blocks of nature.

All this of course takes as much time to flit through my head as it takes me to untangle the hound's leash from around an alder bush, recently decimated by Mrs or Mr. Beaver. We step back into the cool woods, skirt the now-abandoned nest the young ducks came running out of but a few weeks ago, the eggs leftovers still of great interest to the hound.

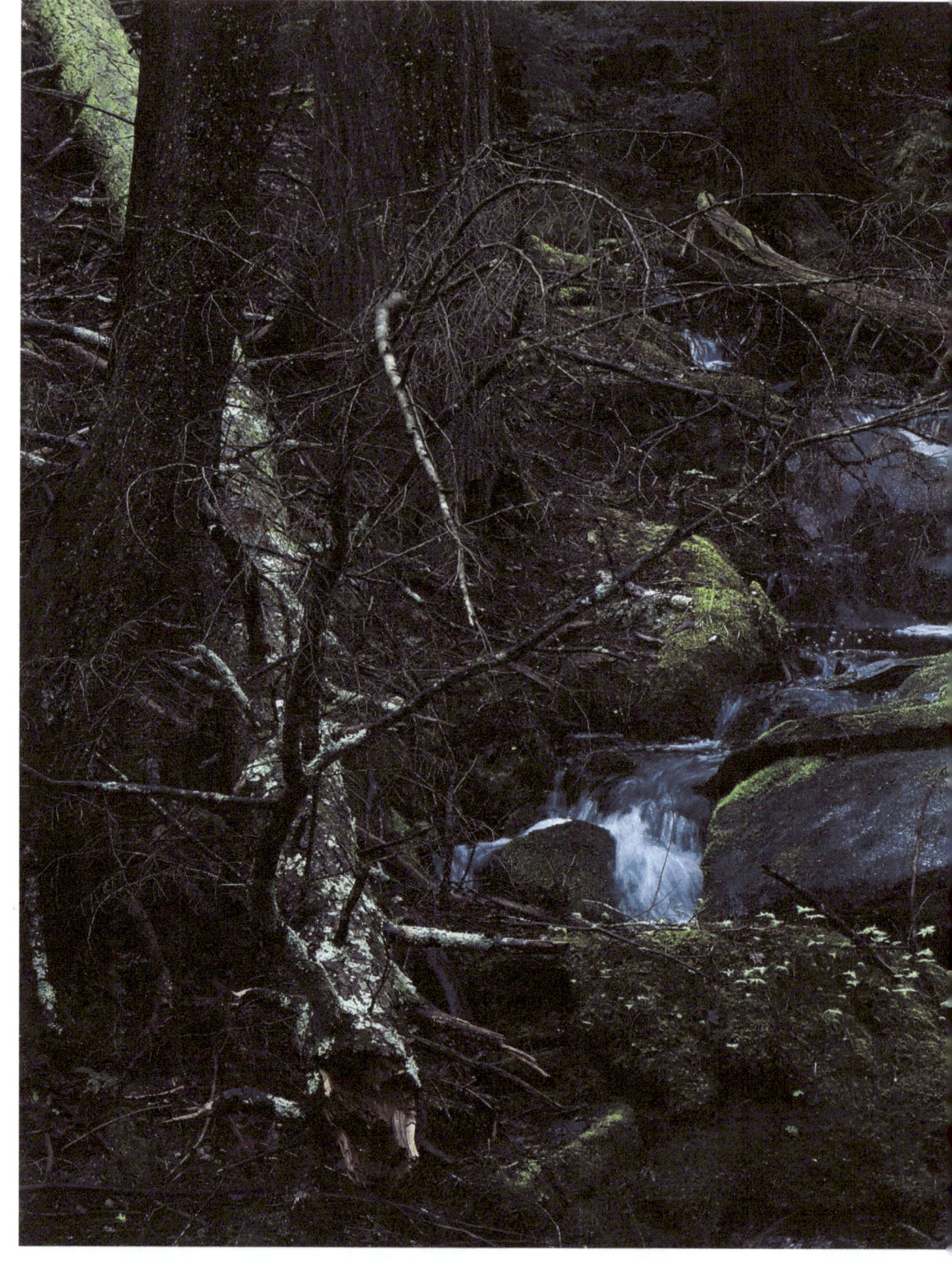

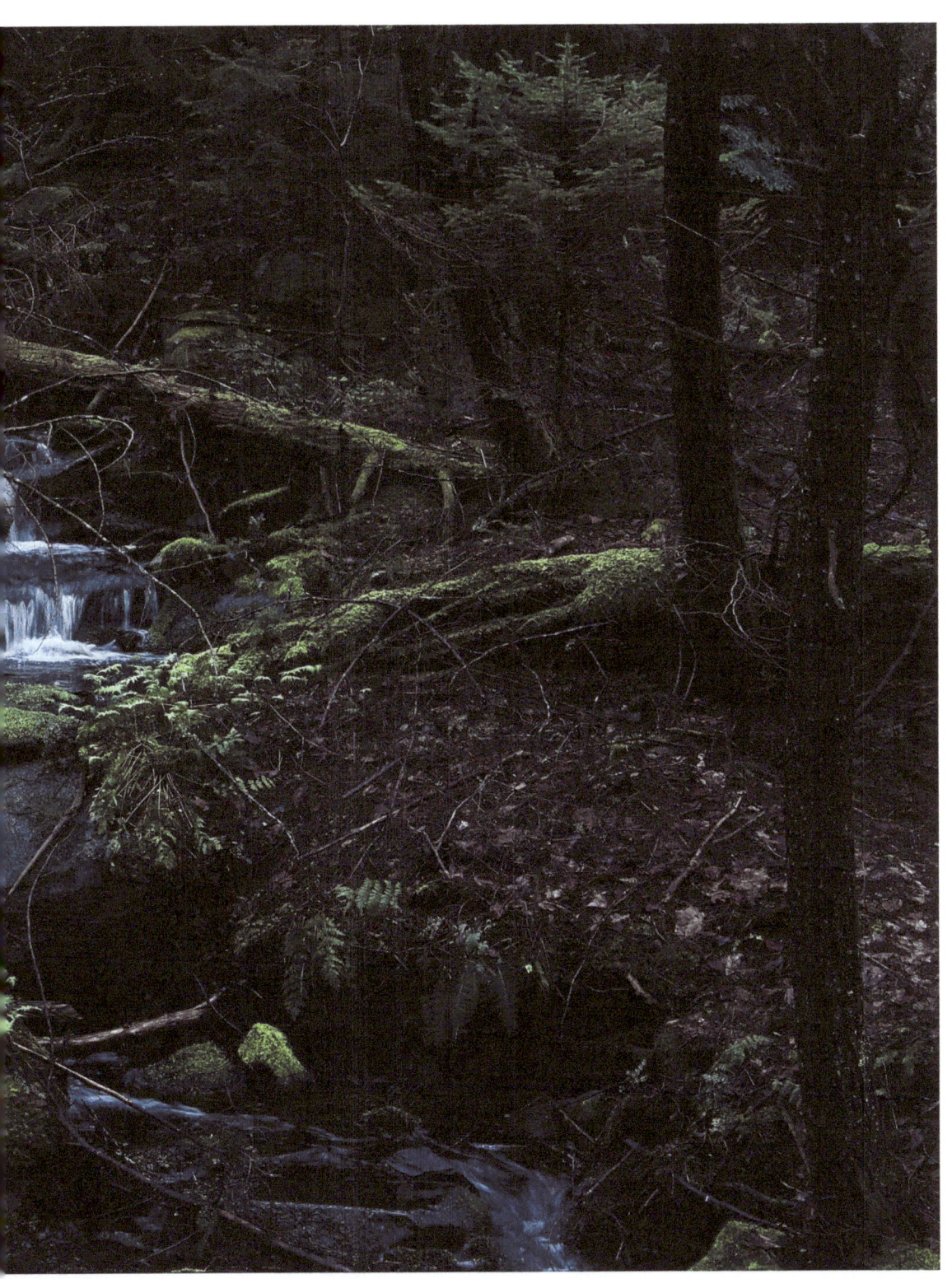

THE LUSTY MONTH OF MAY

In May when every lusty heart flourisheth and bourgeoneth,
for as the season is lusty to behold and comfortable,
so man and woman rejoice and gladden of summer
coming with his fresh flowers: for winter with his rough
winds and blasts causeth a lusty man and woman to cower
and sit fast by the fire.

— *Le Morte d'Arthur, Book 20, ch. 1*

Contrary to what you'd expect, the world gets silent in May. As I walk, a veery of late returned form Brazil sings his exuberant metallic reverberation, on the left up in the canopy. Behind and below, a woodpecker taps a tree.

And yet, quiet peace wraps itself around me. I hear no road sounds, no airplanes, no distant neighbors mowing/sawing/ shooting/barking. The world's in flames and at odds, nature is at riot trying to reproduce itself at lightning speed, but here, around me, all is serenity. May mornings are quiet.

I think this is a miracle served up to me by my brain. Believe you me, the sounds of civilization are happening all around me. A while ago investing in a microphone to record nature sounds seemed like a good idea. Not so much, as it turned out.

It is early in the morning. Very early. A wild Agatha is standing stock still at the edge of a swamp, holding out her phone-cum-fancy mike, ready to record the perfectitude of frogs croaking, a hound swooshing through the water, a tiny tinker stream

tinkling. But the right moment of quiet seldom comes, there's a truck, and airplane, a chainsaw. She may be there, still, for all I know, trying to get it right.

We don't hear the airplanes consciously most of the time, but it's a continuous coming and going overhead, and the sound contributes to our sense of things happening. And since drivers discovered the nearby county road that is a happening place, too.

Not to even mention my ever-busy neighbors with more machines than any one person should have a right to own (I am not innocent of this).

I can't imagine that everyone suddenly decided to go elsewhere or choose another moment. Nor has my hearing gone as much downhill as the world is wont to assume at a certain age.

No, this happens every May, only to repair (?) itself miraculously right around when June 1 rolls around with the return of sound pollution.

I think the birds' insistence focuses my brain. It's not something I do, it just happens. They sing and call their mates, and my evolution-dominated brain pays attention to them and not to all the annoyances. I bet if I were to haul out the mike I'd find that my recordings of the bird sounds are flawed despite the silence I experience.

It's a miracle!

I could wax technical or philosophical on subconscious selective interpretation, but I am not going to question it. Why mess with perfection? That same brain has served me up all the above in about 30 seconds, and now I am free to spend the rest of my allotted hour in solitude in the woods walking and taking photographs and generally bathing in serenity.

And then it's time to check up on the vernal pool. The water is down some, but not as much as we'd feared. There are a few final egg masses working their way towards fruition as tadpoles. They are almost on dry land and it's good they have their protective blob of gelatin.

It's a perfect opportunity for a photograph if you're willing to get your boots pretty muddy and maybe sink in over the rims. I step forward, pressing my itty-bitty waterproof point-and-shoot up to the gelatinous mass because the macro lens on my shiny new camera doesn't do it in such low light. (Not if you're of a certain age and wobbling around in a mud puddle and can't hold it still.)

WHOOSH!! BONG! SPLAT!!

WHAT? *WHAT?*

It's my new camera flying out of its bag into the muck as I bend forward to get nice and close to the blobs of frog and salamander... Nooooooooo.

So much for serenity.

You can dress her up with nice gear, but you can't take her anywhere. She may take off her shirt to start drying her camera.

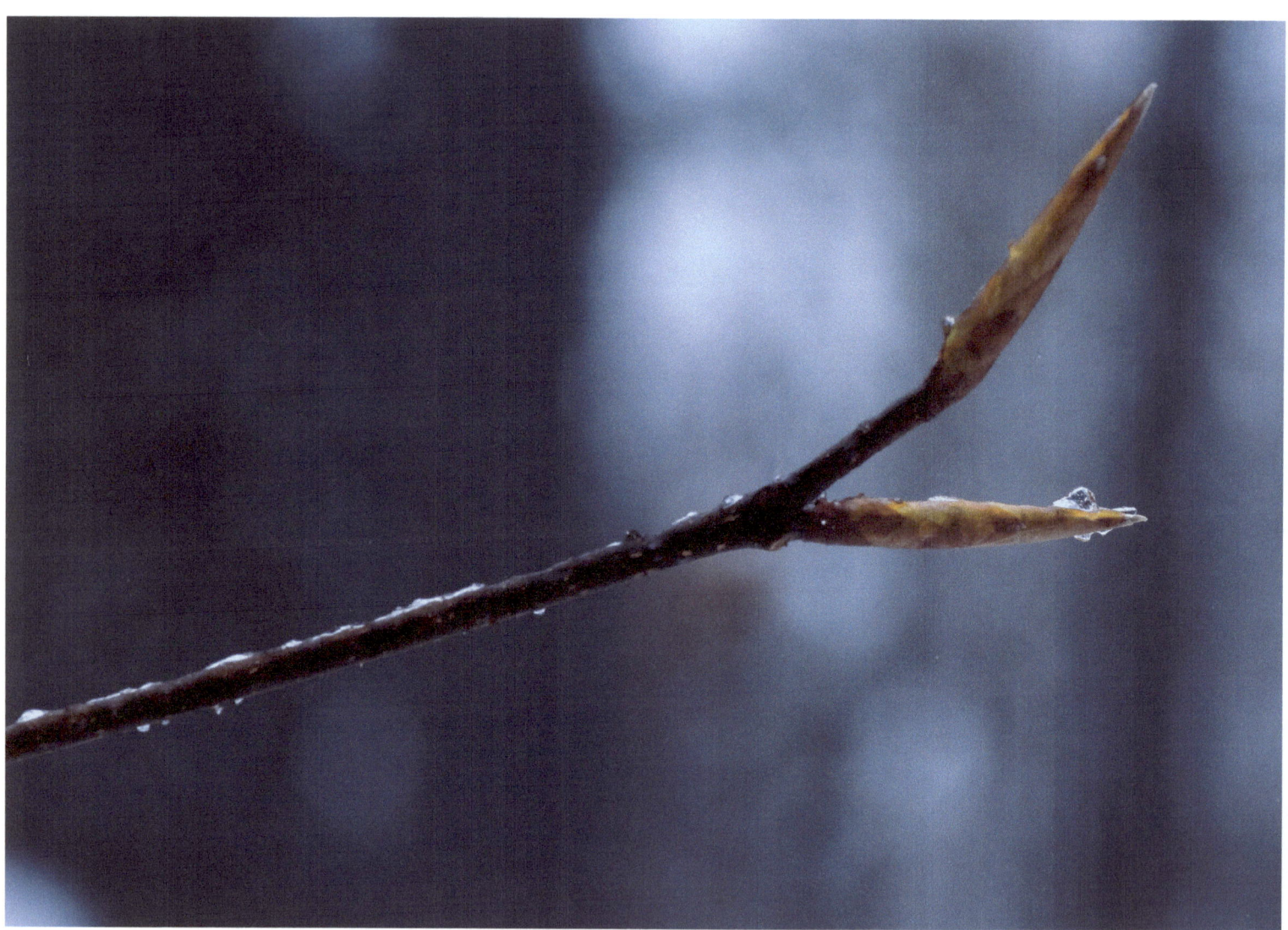

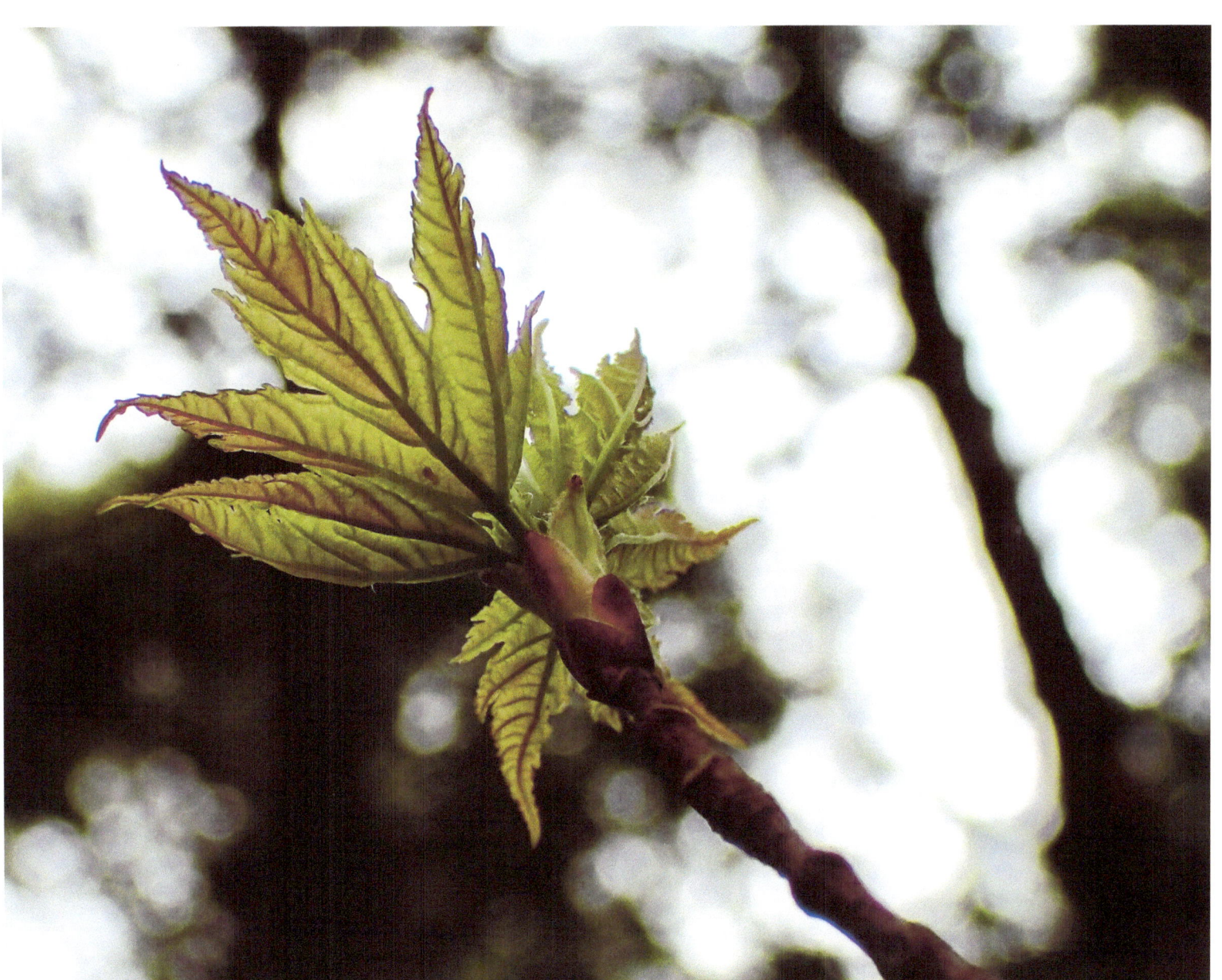

I long dreamt to live here in the forest at the end of a dirt road in the lee of West Mountain. Where the worst of the winter winds swoosh high overhead, the Spotted Spring Salamander thrives, the pines are tall and the stream tinkles all year?

Clearing the brambles out of the depression Dave made with his excavator when he was digging holes for the percolation test for the septic system for the house we never built, I start to think about advertising this land when I have to put it up for sale, maybe next year. I'll definitely mention that it perced beautifully a decade and a half ago.

But this protected and quiet southern slope, enough acreage to spare if you want cut yourself a pretty view, is more than a just a lot to park your designer house on.

"Mila Stetson's place" it was called on a 1938 deed, the house now a a half-cellar hole on the corner of a maple-lined road in the woods to an old apple orchard. The foundation is surrounded by day lilies a chimney base and a pile of chimney bricks made in Plainfield, and the closed-up well we found just exactly where you'd expect it, 10 feet off the rear corner of the house.

All of which would be pretty interesting to someone who has the wherewithal to bring back the sense of the old place — so you can enjoy it by looking and feeling, instead of just knowing it's there and seeing it in your mind's eye like I have been doing for twenty years.

Levi Stetson was born in 1803. His father, Levi (who was known as Levi Stetson, Junior), and his family moved to Plainfield in 1807, along with the rest of poor to middling Abington, MA, it seems. The Abington crowd thought they had a good idea by the tail. All that water tumbling down, plenty of wood, roads being built. Better access to the West than perhaps more southerly and northerly.

In 1824, with his eye on the main chance, "our" Levi got married. I don't know exactly when he bought and built his farm, but he chose well. It is on a South-facing slope, suitable for grazing sheep, near a small, fast-flowing stream suitable for damming for a mill, right on the stage road that leads across Savoy Mountain to Albany. Or did then. He may have expected to do make mark, along with his new wife, Sarah.

Unfortunately, it was not to be. The bottom fell out of the New England wool market soon after they settled, the railroads went elsewhere, and small water-powered mills became a thing of the past over the course of the nineteenth century.

There are signs of mill works on the brook but very few right here. When Levi died in 1879 he left behind 75 acres and a house of which the cellar hole had never been finished, suggesting that he had not been particularly successful, in a town that had been losing population since he came of age.

Sarah had died some time earlier. Mila, Levi's second wife of only six years lived on his farm for another fifteen, and her name became attached to the "home farm."

The Stetson kids sold it all to cousin Sarah Stetson as soon as Mila moved to Northampton in 1895, where she died in 1899, perhaps at the State Hospital. Sarah's son Alvah, a life long bachelor, moved in and in due time he came to own the farm.

Land is expensive to own, especially if you can't make it produce, and the Depression was a hard hit. In 1938 Alvah Stetson deeded his homestead and other land to Reginald Burbank, a New York physician who made his money with the then-new and now forgotten 'gold cure" for rheumatism.

By that time, all the grand ideas of farming were past. Alvah relinquished title for back taxes (conjecture) and the right to live out his life on the place, cut wood, have boarders after seeking permission, and fish the new pond he may have created for Burbank.

The doctor wanted a small kingdom to fish in and bought up hundreds upon hundreds of acres in Plainfield, taking down a number of houses so as to lower his own tax burden and letting the forest take back the fields.

Since all things must pass so did his fortune as Burbank and his second wife Kathryn Poole reportedly huddled in their unheated Fifth Avenue Mansion, taking options on their kingdom in Plainfield to make a buck, not delivering in the main, except to the New Jersey man who forced them to sell some hundreds of acres just west of here.

And Poole's daughter after him was so just the same that she stuck me with a bill for back taxes when I bought this land twenty years ago to make my homestead.

All of those shenanigans brought us land that wasn't touched for a long time, land with majestic white pines that swoosh in the wind coming off the mountain. A babbling brook that, one way or another, provided the Pixley neighbors with water for their mill just down the street. Thousands of acres of Audubon land just up the road, one neighbor away in any direction. No cars coming by.

Land where two of my dogs lie, land crossed by a private road lined with maples. And where, when I still my infernal whacker, it is so quiet I resolve to eat dry bread rather than to let it go, this land that fueled my dreams of building a house and making my future in Plainfield.

Having settled elsewhere in town, I still have some dreaming in me, and should it come to pass that I can, would I not want to build a little place to work here?

Who will next dream to live here in the forest at the end of a dirt road in the lee of West Mountain where the worst of the winter winds swoosh high overhead and the Spotted Spring Salamander thrives?

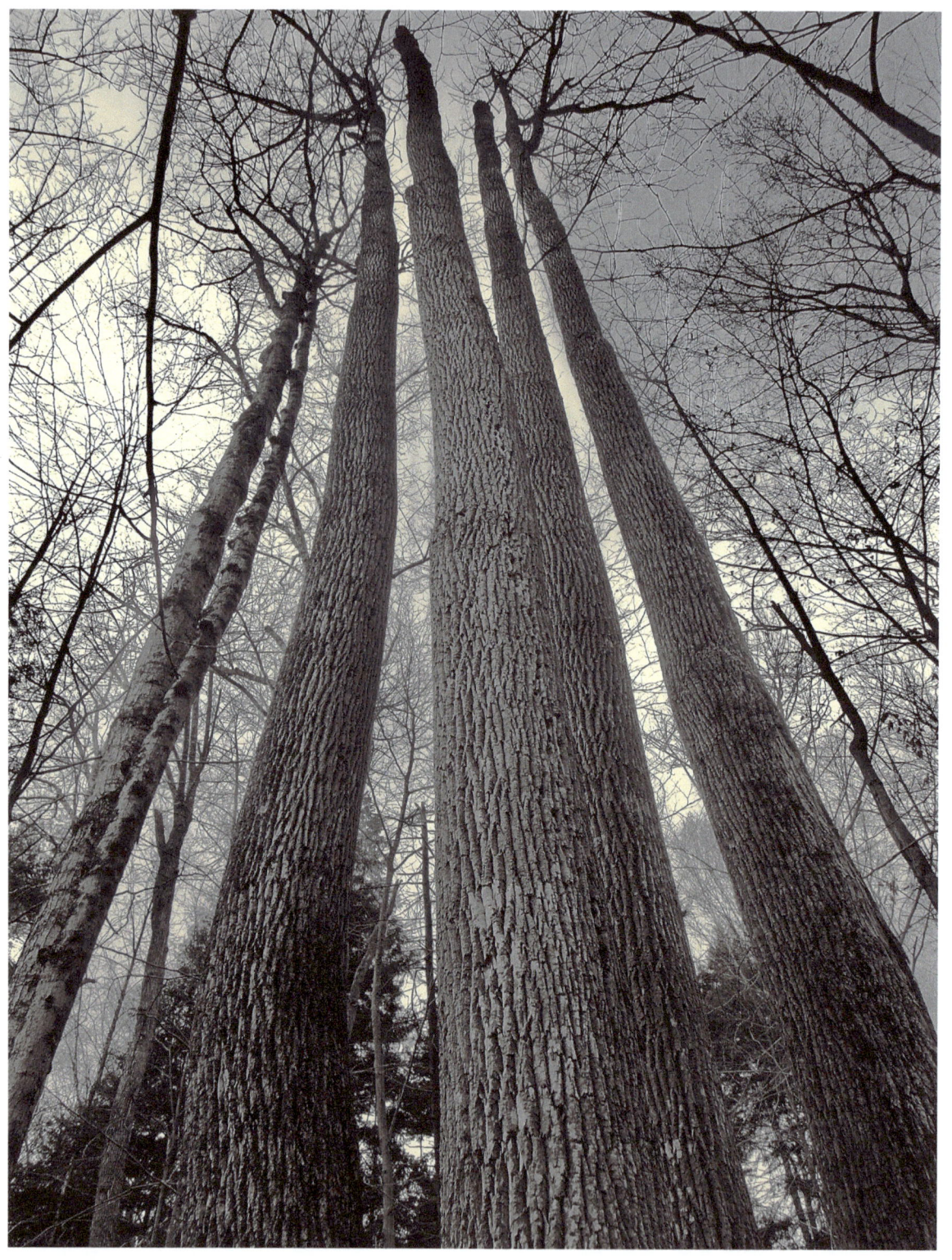

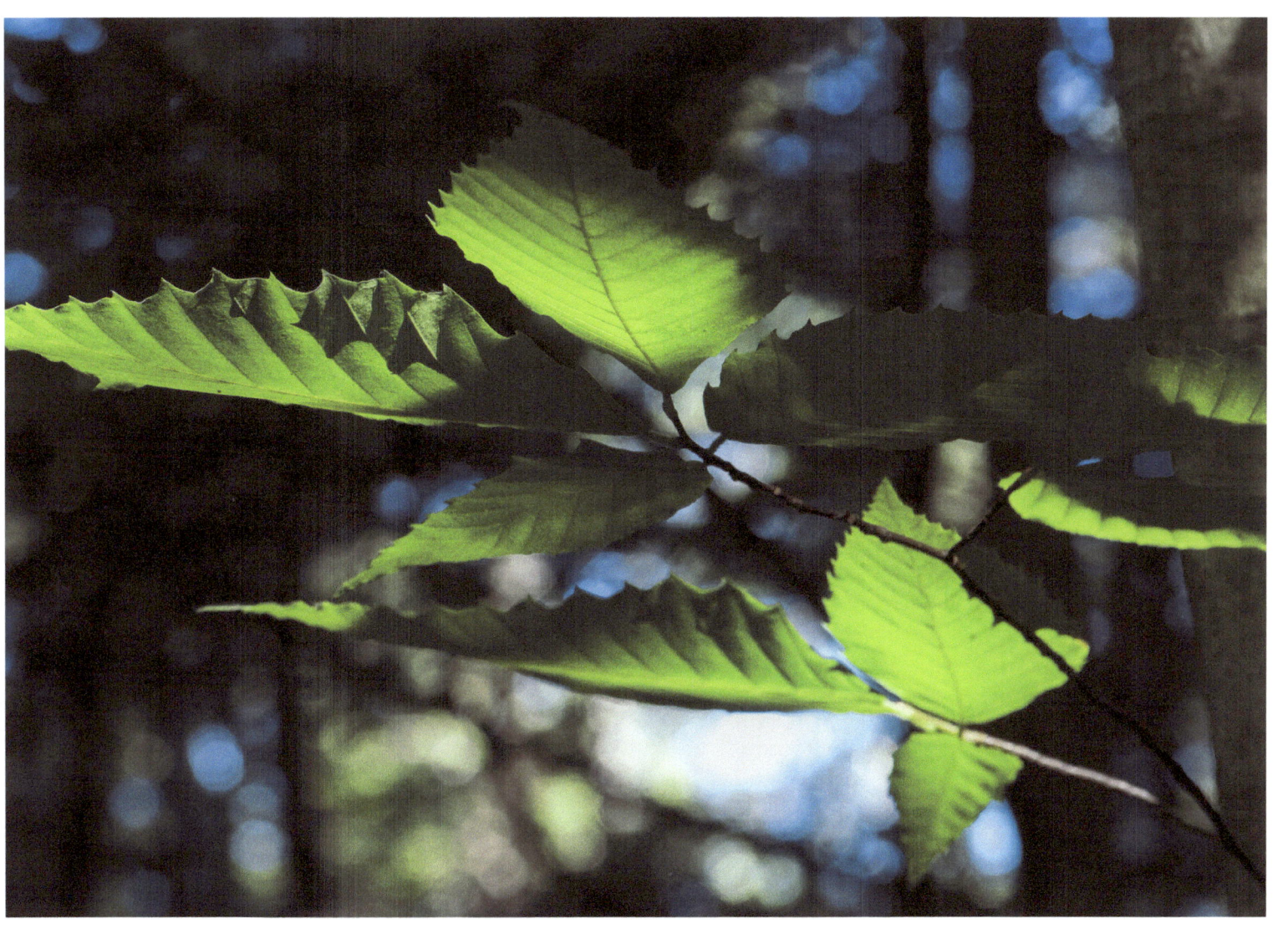

It rains so you'd notice only once in a while, this year. But when it rains, especially in this long slow autumn, the world bursts out into being: woods and walls are suddenly intensely and three-dimensionally painted in strong pigments, smells of pine and autumn leaves bring a nostalgic wish to simply lie down and inhale, and everything glimmers and shimmers and reflects the light of the sky.

Even all the drips and drops and plinks of water on wood and on stone and on water tap insistently on the window of my consciousness: "I am here, pay attention to me, listen, this is real, you need to pay attention."

The next morning as I read the the rain gauge, clouds start to race and the air clears. Our morning walk is filled with the whooshing of wind high in the trees. Air so crisp you can smell it as clearly as the earthy scents that just took wing.

At which point I am encountering, in the words from the last paragraph of *The Great Gatsby*, the "fresh green breast of the new world" and it is the start of a new adventure:

I became aware of the old island here that flowered once for Dutch sailors' eyes — a fresh, green breast of the new world. Its vanished trees, the trees that had made way for Gatsby's house, had once

*pandered in whispers to the last and greatest of all human dreams; for a **transitory** enchanted moment man must have held his breath in the presence of this continent, compelled into an aesthetic contemplation he neither understood nor desired, face to face for the last time in history with something commensurate to his capacity for wonder.*

And I marvel at my own ability to take on the wonder of the Dutch sailors rather than the disappointment of the "Valley of the Ashes" Fitzgerald describes so eloquently in his novel, the world of

careless people, [like] Tom and Daisy-[who] smashed up things and creatures and then retreated back into their money or their vast carelessness, or whatever it was that kept them together, and let other people clean up the mess they had made.

Now, perhaps as much as anytime before we started cleaning up the worst messes of the industrial revolution, we are elevating carelessness to an art form. And yet, one sniff and I am transported into a time when we had not yet transformed a continent.

No matter how much I try to use less plastic, and all the rest of it, like Nick and like Gatsby, I keep my eyes on the lights at the ends of the docks across the bay rather than on the ashes I, too, pile up behind me. I wonder what it will take.

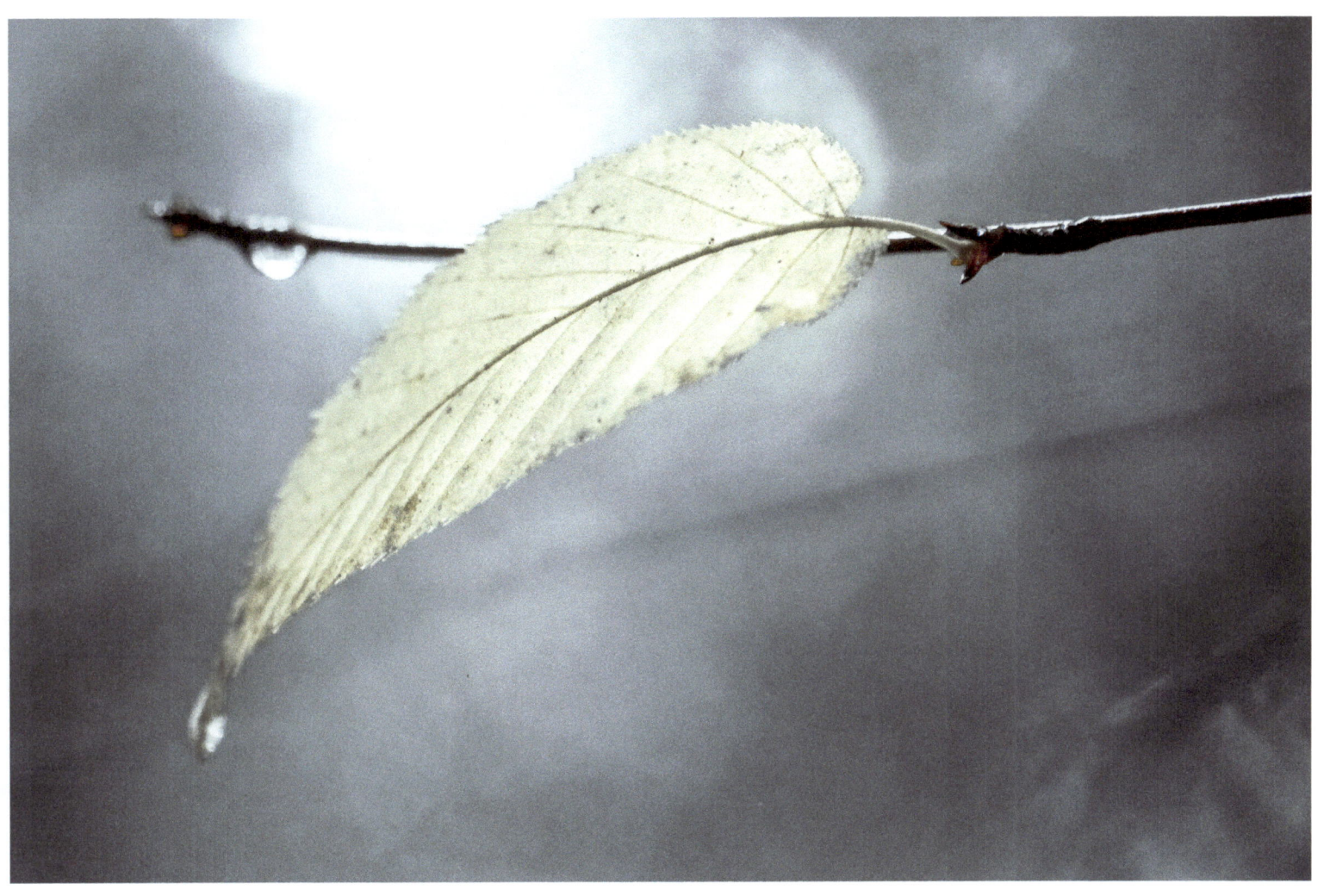

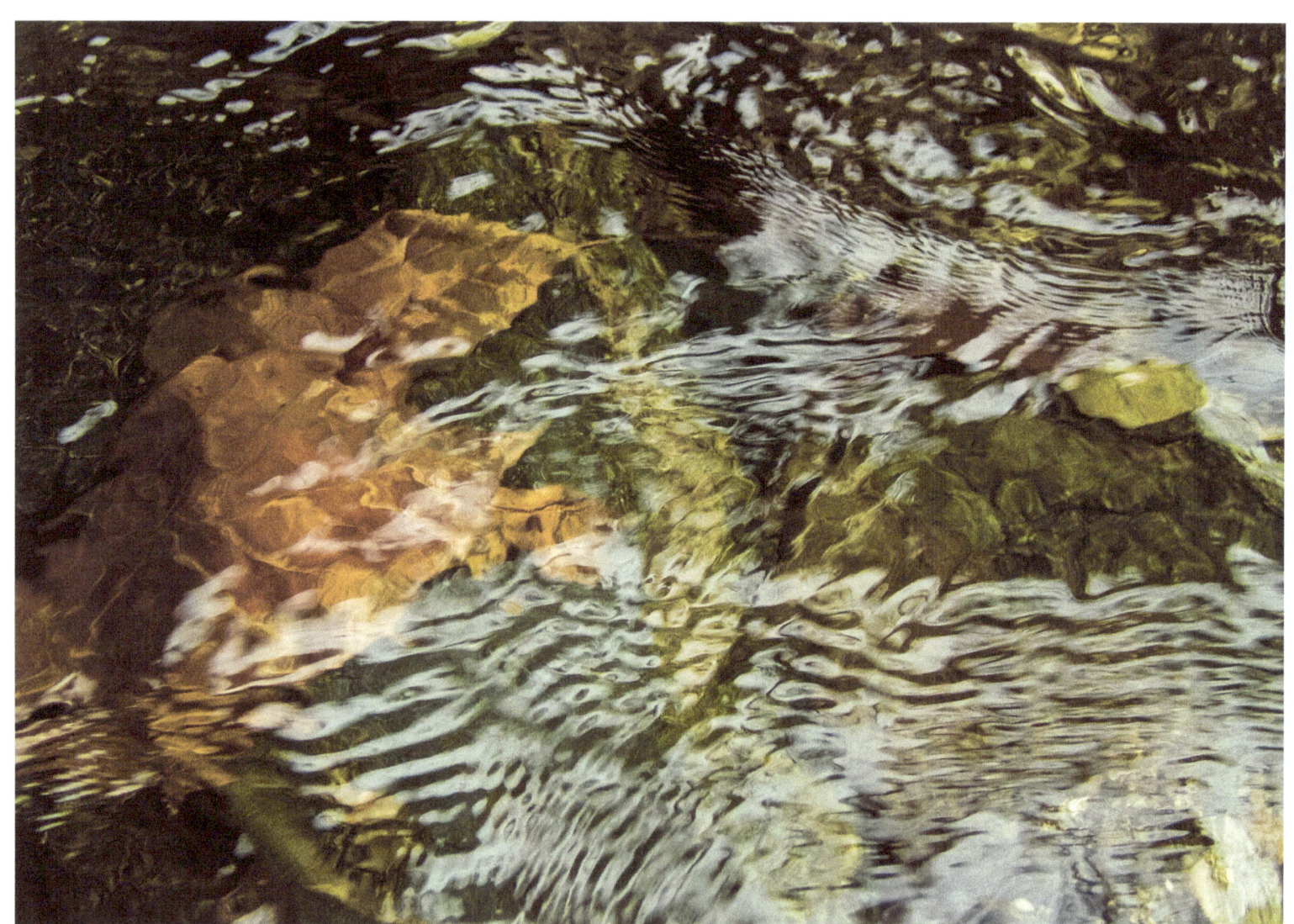

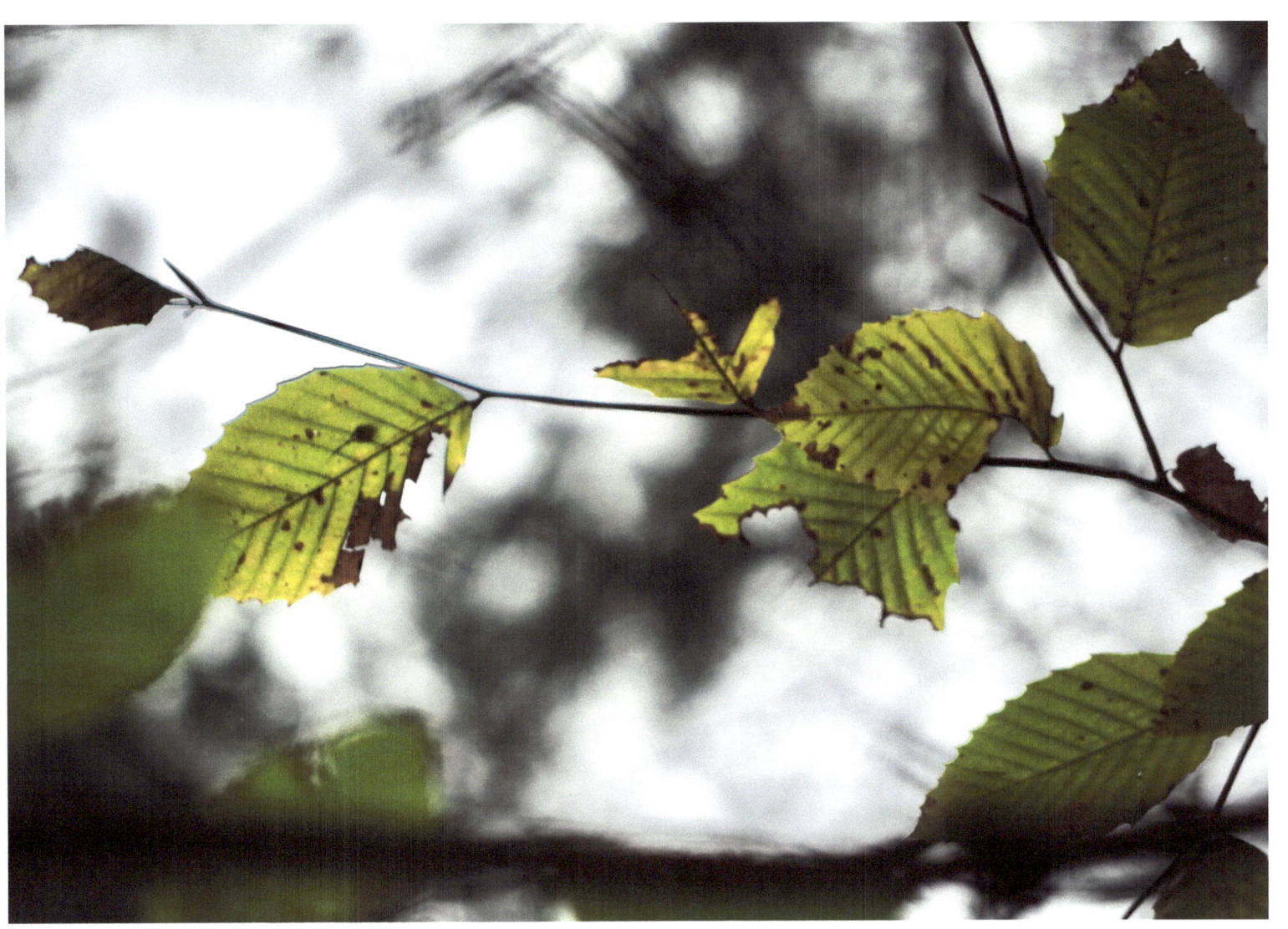

Don't mind me, I am just out here chasing a leaf. Desperately trying to catch one on its way down as it is about to hit my camera. Not happening.

I can't see the leaf without focusing the lens and the lens can't keep up with the speed of the leaf coming down. It's not a stone, that's true, but gravity still does its work once a leaf is on its way down.

You do know what gravity does, insofar as it exists?* It speeds things up on the way down, accelerating all the way. Stone or leaf, same difference. It doesn't matter how heavy it is — if you drop a couch, a pebble, and a mafioso off a roof they will hit the pavement at the same time. No difference. You don't want any of them falling on your head at that speed.

What does make a difference is the resistance of the air. There's not much mass in a leaf getting ready for fall. It's is a bit dried out, the cells don't hold water that well any longer, so it makes a nice sail. All it needs is the movement of air up or down a slope, never mind any wind.

Thus, it would be best to get the leaf on your head. Which is sort of what I am trying for and where they tend to land after I fail to catch them on sensor.

From one of the best books I've ever read, *The Forest Unseen* by David Haskell, I found out that trees have a specific footprint depending how far their leaves and seeds sail. Some are better than others at using the thermals to get places, following hawks high overhead performing loop-de-loops on the updraft from the ridge just up the hill across the road.

The other day I thought I had found the perfect leaf to follow, photogenically orange and taking its time on the way down. I was ready, having worked out yet another way in which I might catch it with the camera. And then it disappeared.

Presently I found it again, merrily surfing the updrafts over into another tree, pausing there but for a moment to visit a branch and then lifting up on monarch wings and soaring above the tops of the trees before wending its way downslope towards the bog. I never did get to say goodbye, it was too busy getting as high as it could.

You may have some trouble ahead or behind, but being out here, chasing a leaf, brings you right back to the business of being. So don't mind me, I am just out there stalking a leaf, or surfing the updraft as the case may be.

* Gravity does not exist, says science. Fine, it's only a way of talking about things falling. But it works as a concept here on earth, so I am sticking with it until I have a concept that works better at explaining what's happening around me.

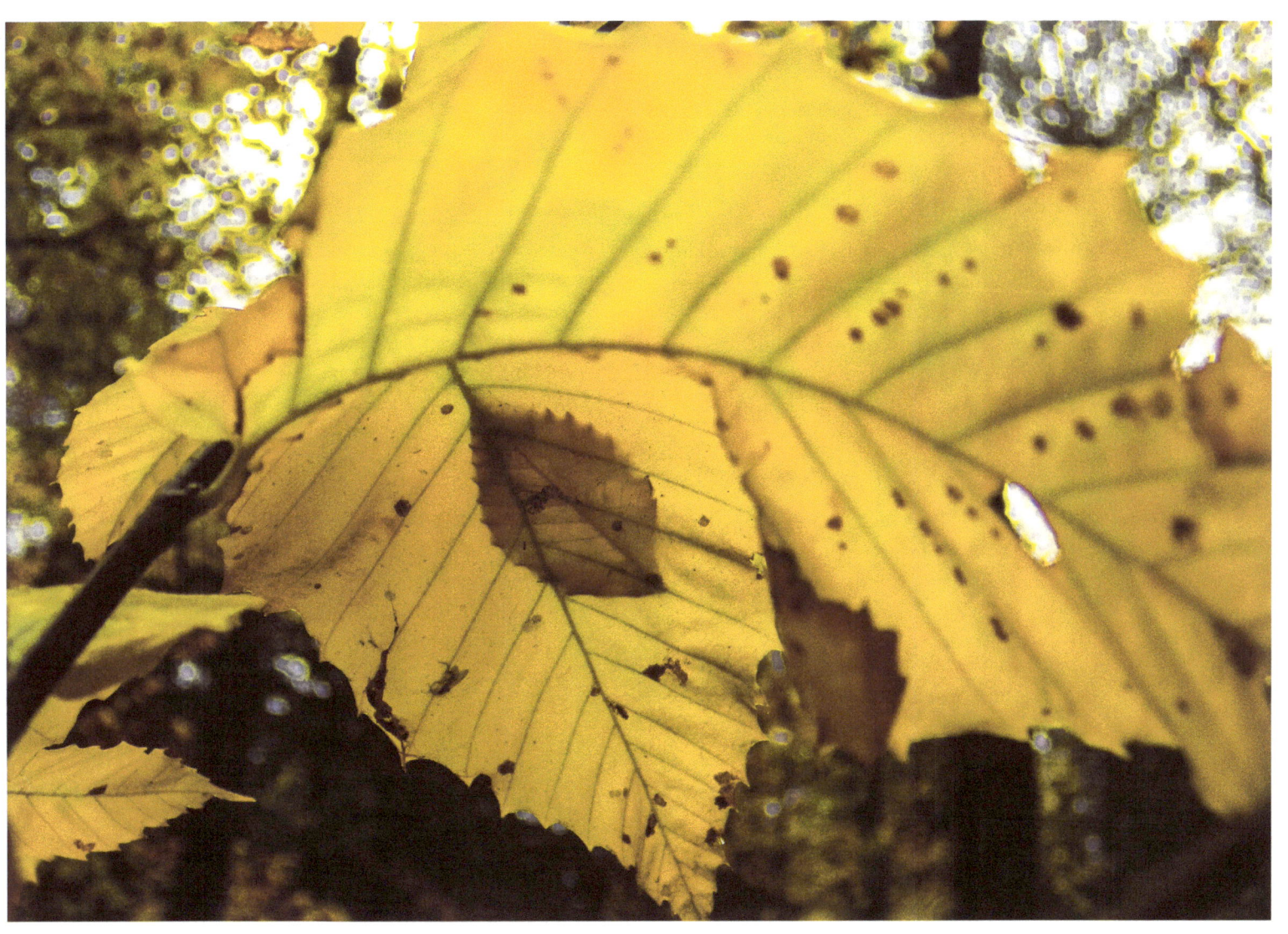

If you are lucky, you may find yourself walking down a country lane in late autumn on a slightly broody morning, when the wind picks up high in the trees and the clouds break up just enough to let the sun catch the leaves swirling down from the tall tall maples and poppels and beeches lining the lane.

And when you do, you and your hound and your love may stand still in awe and crane your necks and then turn giddy with the richness of it all and try to catch leaves whichever way you know how and tell each other how great this is and to keep this moment forever in whichever way you can.

Okay, not the hound. The hound is busy sniffing at the base of the trees to find out where the errant squirrel may best be intercepted. His world is smell.

———

As a species we appear to be mainly experiential just like a dog chasing a squirrel or a blowing leaf: we respond to that which we can see, smell, feel, hear, to that what is now rather than in the future. That which we know happens but we don't directly feel on our bodies or in our wallets is off stage.

For one thing, we largely ignore the incredible process of vast amounts of biological material growing, living, and dying all around us and even inside us, each item an intricate design executed just so. Unless of course it's pretty

and comes swirling into our face. Sure, we see mosquitoes and a few spiders and are moved to banish them from our environment because they are incompatible with our sense of comfort (and many are, who wants lice or fleas? When black flies really go at it they can kill a moose).

But mostly we harness a minuscule amount of it for food and shelter, try to keep a lot of it at bay (removing the wasp nest, raking the falling leaves, clipping the hedge), and ignore the rest although we know it's there and we count on it for the air we breathe. Once in a while, we go for a visit to some special parts of it, the Everglades for instance, and get a thrill from the vague and specific threats out there.

Instead of paying attention to this, we prefer to believe in some unseen force that looks from on high at our doing. In many cases, we have that unseen force give permission to our most base instincts in fattening our wallets or devaluing others so we can control them, because we can't quite keep their individualities and activities at bay by ignoring them or fencing them out, like we do with the pulsing biomass of the planet.

I think we can't stand it that the other biomasses on the planet completely ignore us. It hurts our sense of self importance. Actually seeing them would force us to reorder our priorities.

If the trees were to pay tribute or call us master, would we pay attention to the need to keep them in good shape?

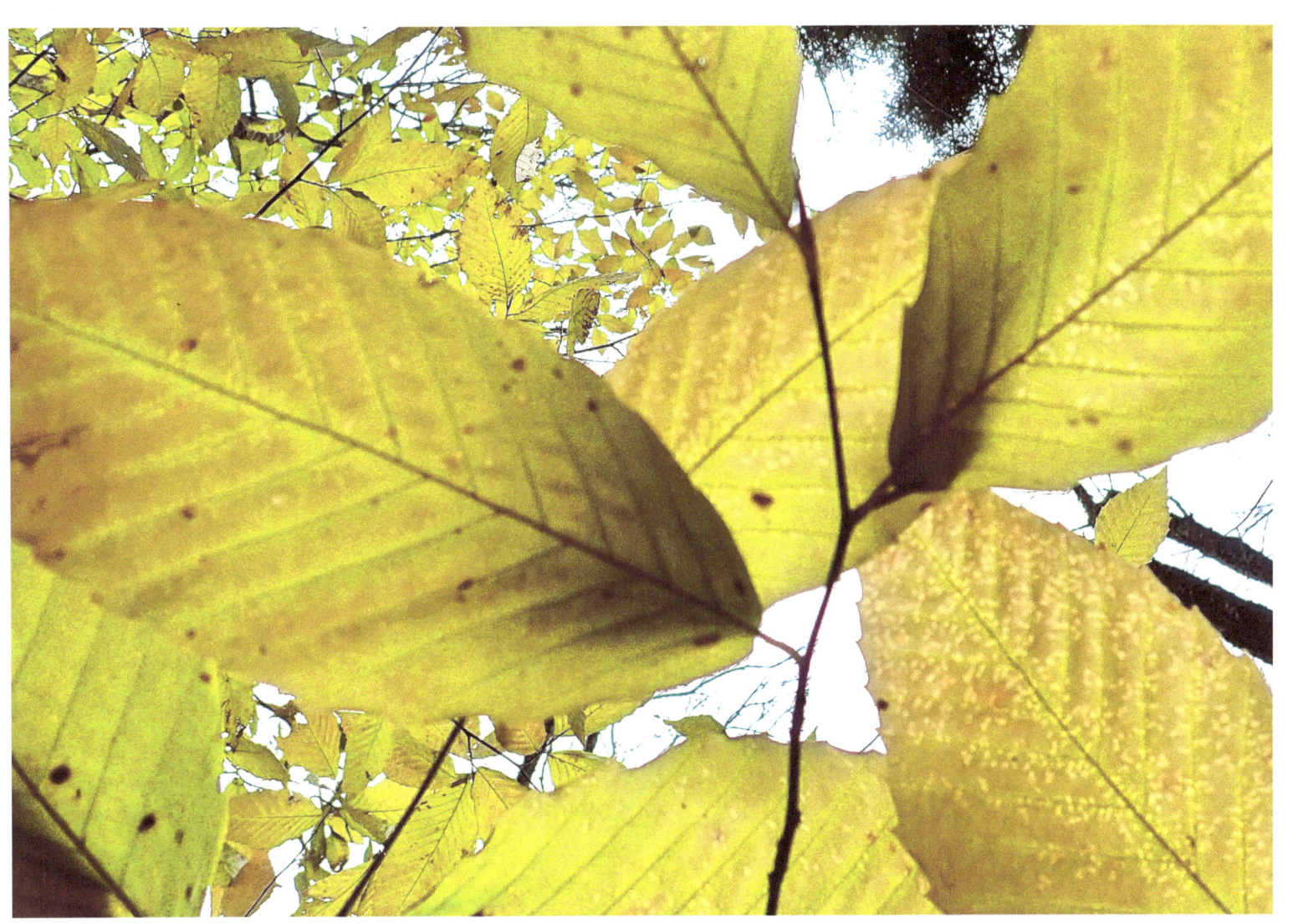

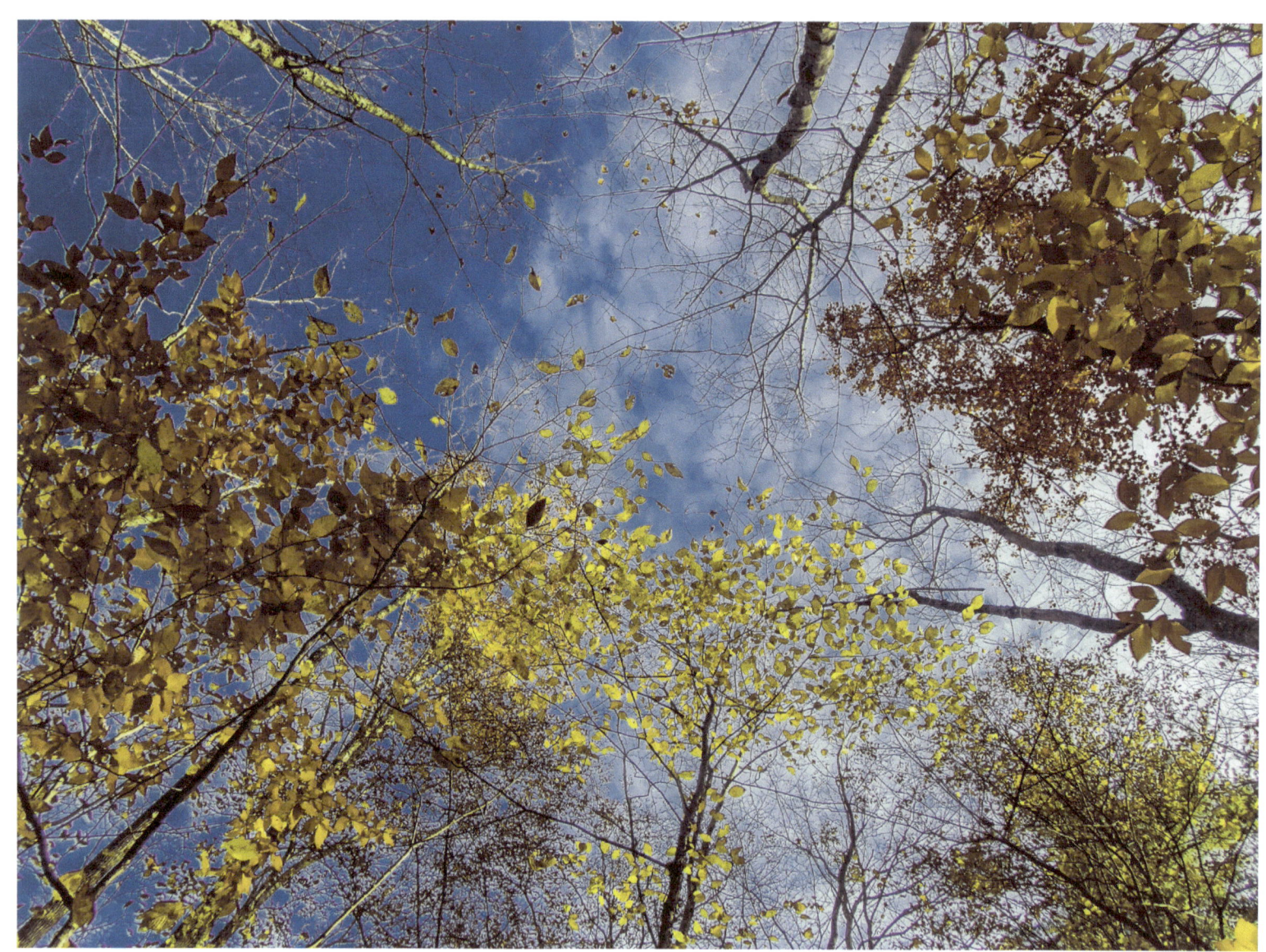

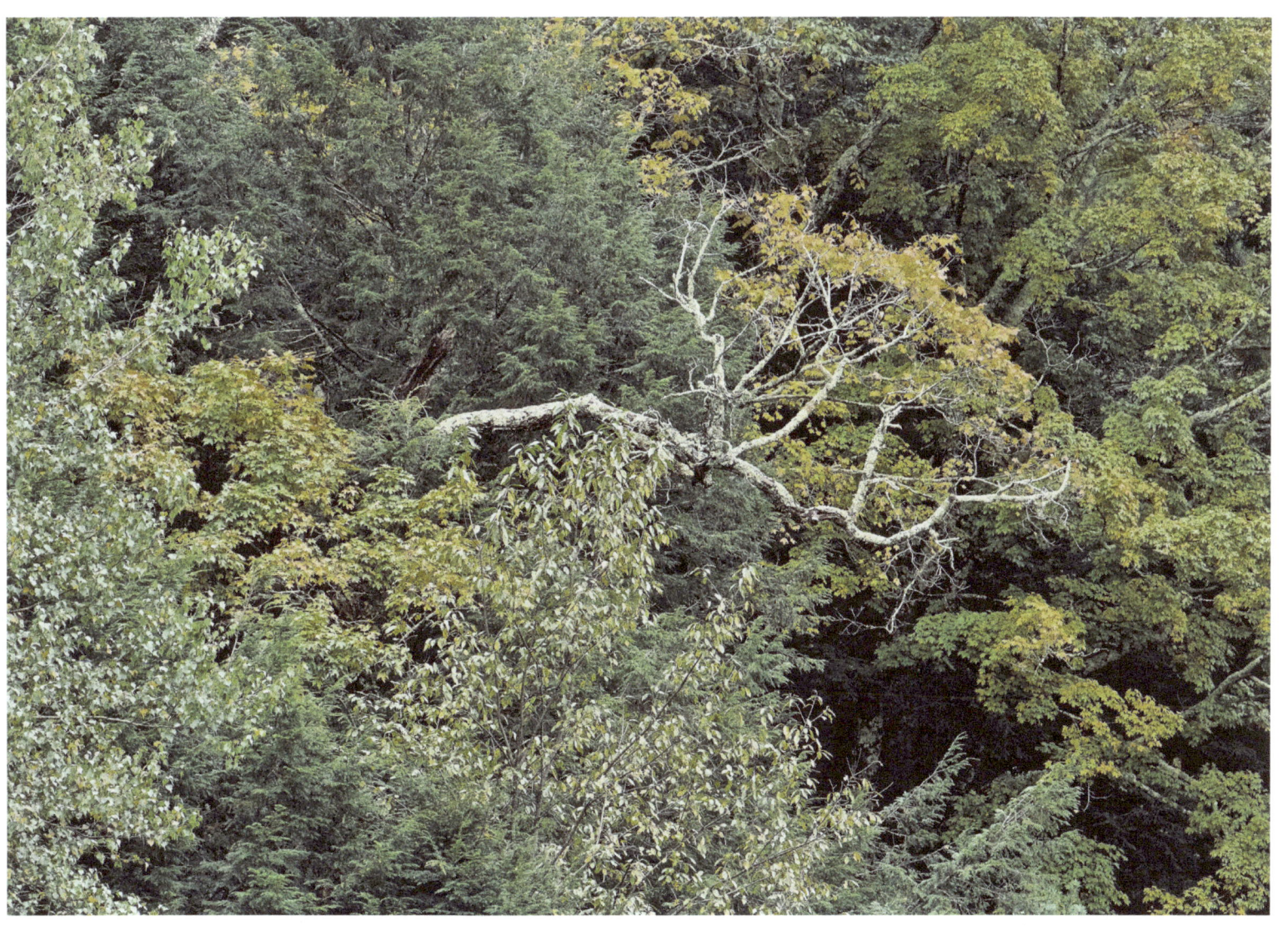

A Snowball's Chance

After the prolonged riot of autumn winter was going to leach saturation from the landscape and bring everything back to basics of shape and shade. Instead, day after day, we gorged on a riot of color in a drenched woods.

Today it's over. Colors are shouting "I'm alive" while disappearing under a very definitive layer of icy snow, itself bringing a new feast to work on next.

As we nervously debate whether this is what we get to expect from climate change and whether there's a snowball's chance in hell that we get out of this alive as a species (will there be oxygen when the trees are all gone?), I think about simply enjoying being out there without the guilt of not doing anything useful to stop it, at least not right at that very moment.

Is feasting on the colors and smells of the boggy wetness that sustains me a way of sticking my head into the mud by kneeling in it? To hell with it, I think, *après nous le deluge*, we must indulge to commit.

She who is missed taught me during 47 years and miles upon miles of adventure that the pleasure of a walk in the park can equal that of an expedition to the Grand Canyon as long as you're willing to jump into each puddle with both feet — and know that there are canyons out there for next year's adventure of course.

Here's hoping….

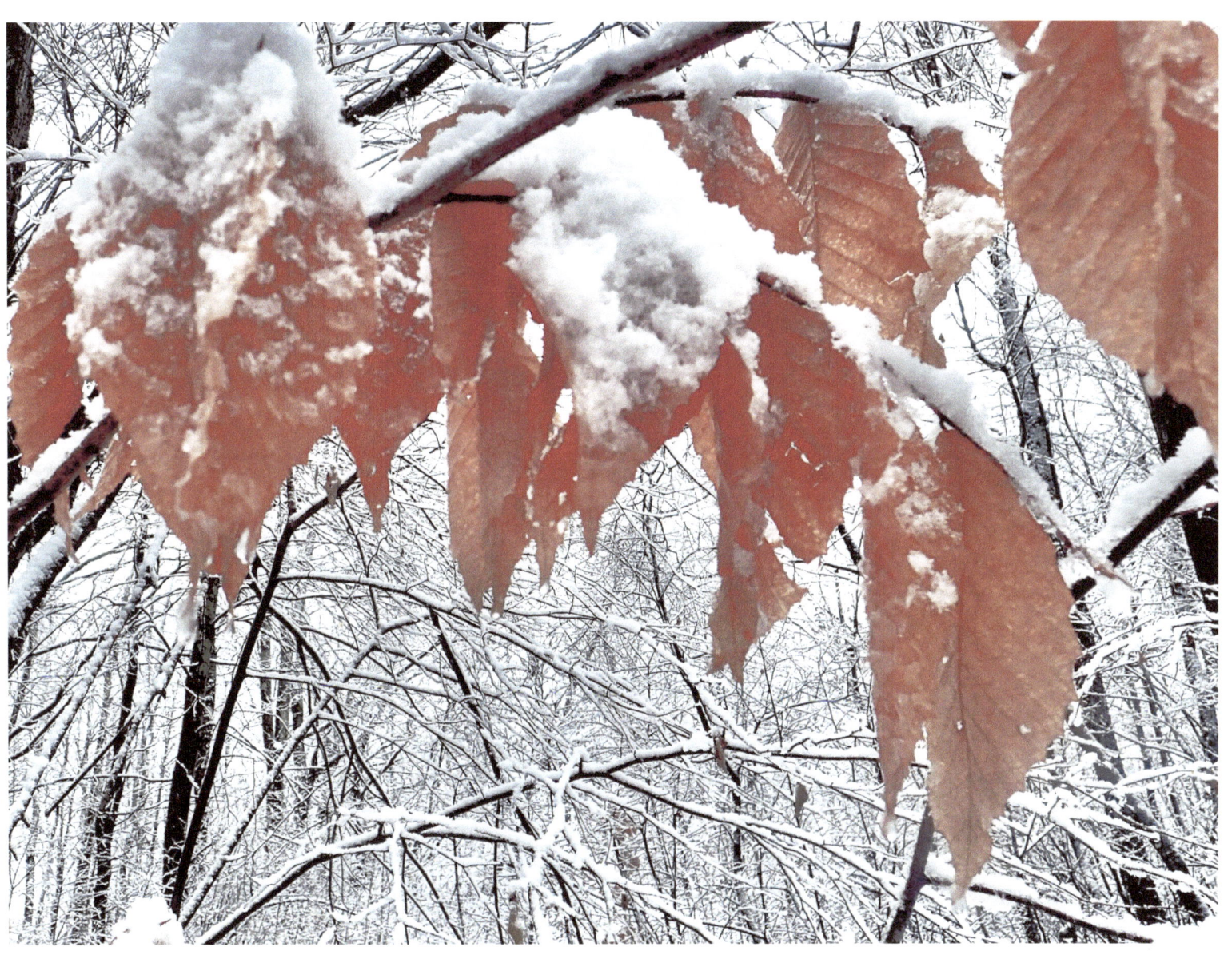

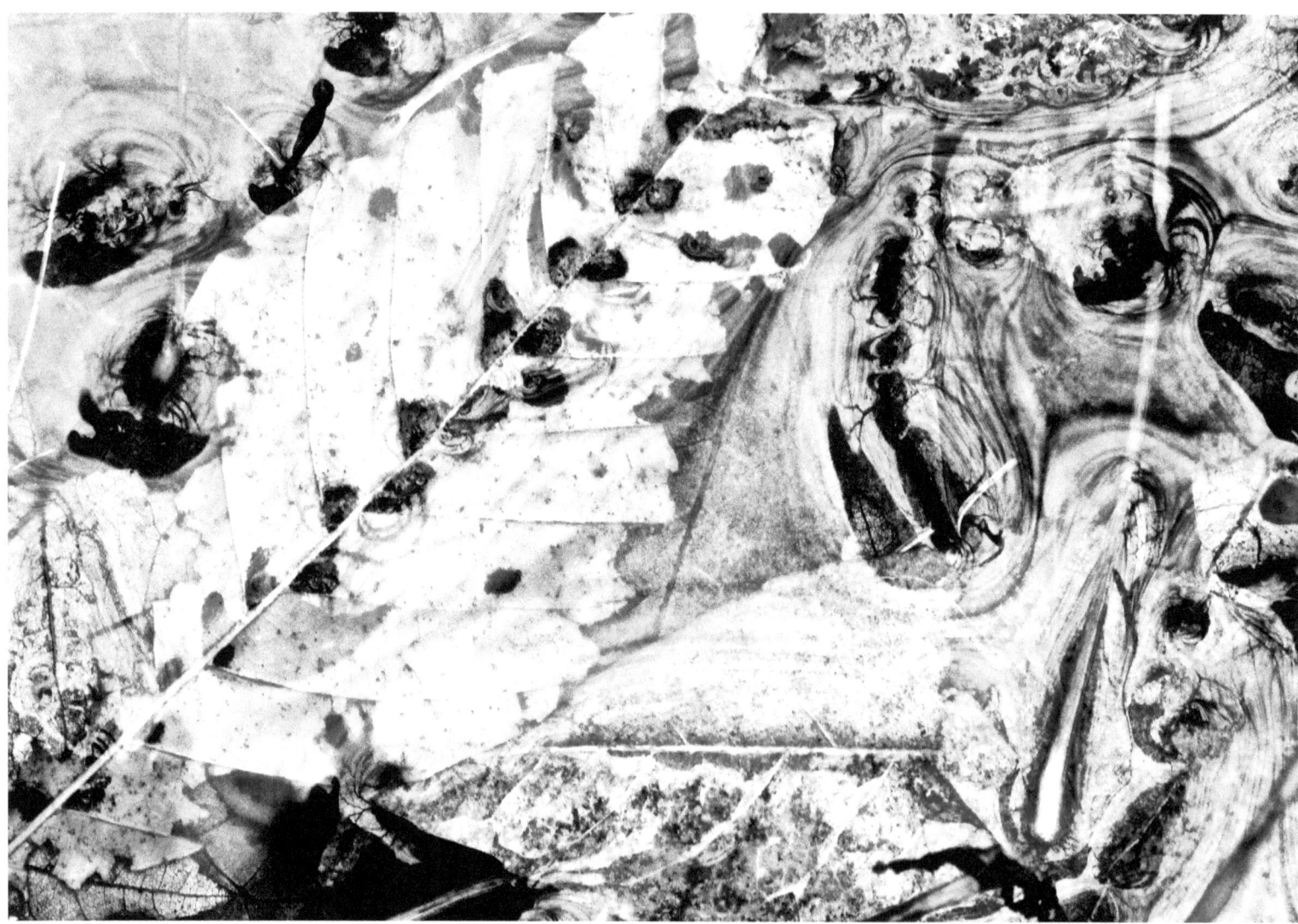

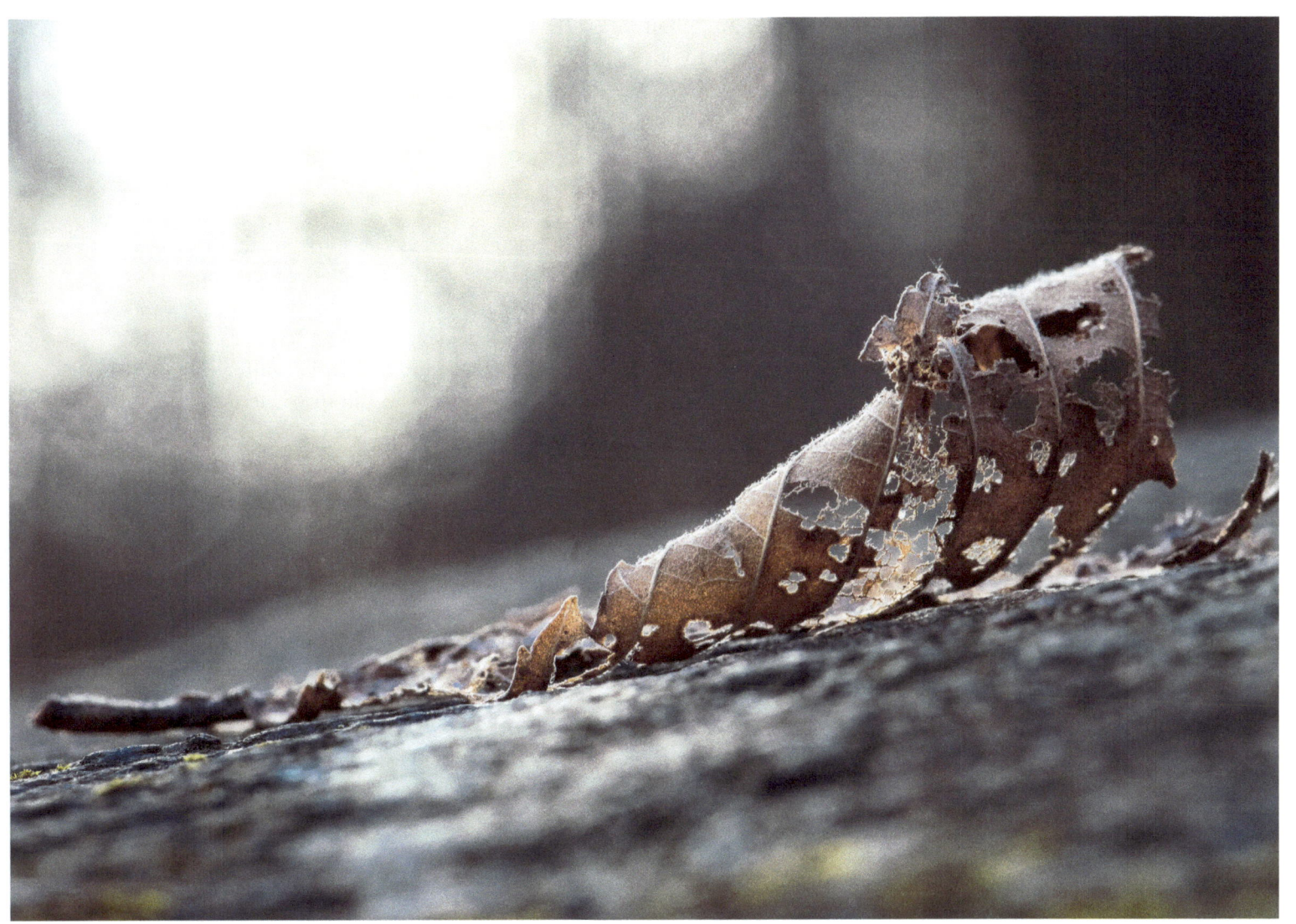

Decorating for the Holidays

A week or two before Christmas the woods come alive. Small tableaus of wood and plant, leaf and stone, shape and color appear to be readying themselves for transport. I want to drag it all inside: the earthy smell, moss, bits of orphaned bark with or without lichen, small dried up mushrooms, and of course the balsam that lures. Rather roughly, I feel up one tree after another, sniffing deeply to gauge how much scent I may have unleashed, trying to imagine this tree in my house.

Where in other years I have futilely tried to find ways to bring the sparkle and shine of ice into a house heated by a wood stove, or to replicate in miniature the charm of a wet and mossy stone wall, this year 's leisurely and damp onset of winter brings me back to the holiday decorating of my childhood in a temperate zone — greens, cones, and berries vie for pride of place with a candle in a small basket.

I wish I could stick my 24 acres into a basket with a candle. Instead, I take photos and walk on, trying to simply become one with this cool freshen goodness and have it always be part of me so I can stop longing for once.

Dragging a tree into the house in the middle of the winter makes eminent sense: preserving the life of the woods just when you don't smell or feel it outside any longer. Bringing greens inside is a longstanding habit in households as removed from us as those of the ancient Egyptians and Romans. It involves keeping evil away, chasing the darkness back whence it came, bridling hope for a greener time.

Pine boughs and pine trees hold a special place in that ritual: not only are they green, they smell clean and freshen things up in the dark and miserable hovels of most of humanity. No wonder Glade and Pine Sol are so dear to our hearts.

In Nordic mythology the spirits of the trees ward off evil but they need to be appeased, too. Getting a tree for the house conveniently chops down two necessary rituals with one axe. We still do it: in construction the workers affix a small tree, bough if necessary, in the skeleton of a house or building when the highest point is reached -- it's called "topping out" and it's a hint that amounts to blackmail.

 It wards off bad luck from the place and it allows the boss to appease the spirits of nature in the guise of the workers by giving them a couple of beers along with it. Prehistoric labor relations. Solve and you're done.

Obviously, I am driven by something deep inside to find green and natural things to freshen up my miserable hovel. It's species memory: not only do I have strong good feelings remembering getting a tree with my mother and hanging all our tools into it to bend the branches down so they would readily receive baubles, but I am ensuring that the light will return.

And while I am at it, I ward off the evil that seems to be hanging over things lately.

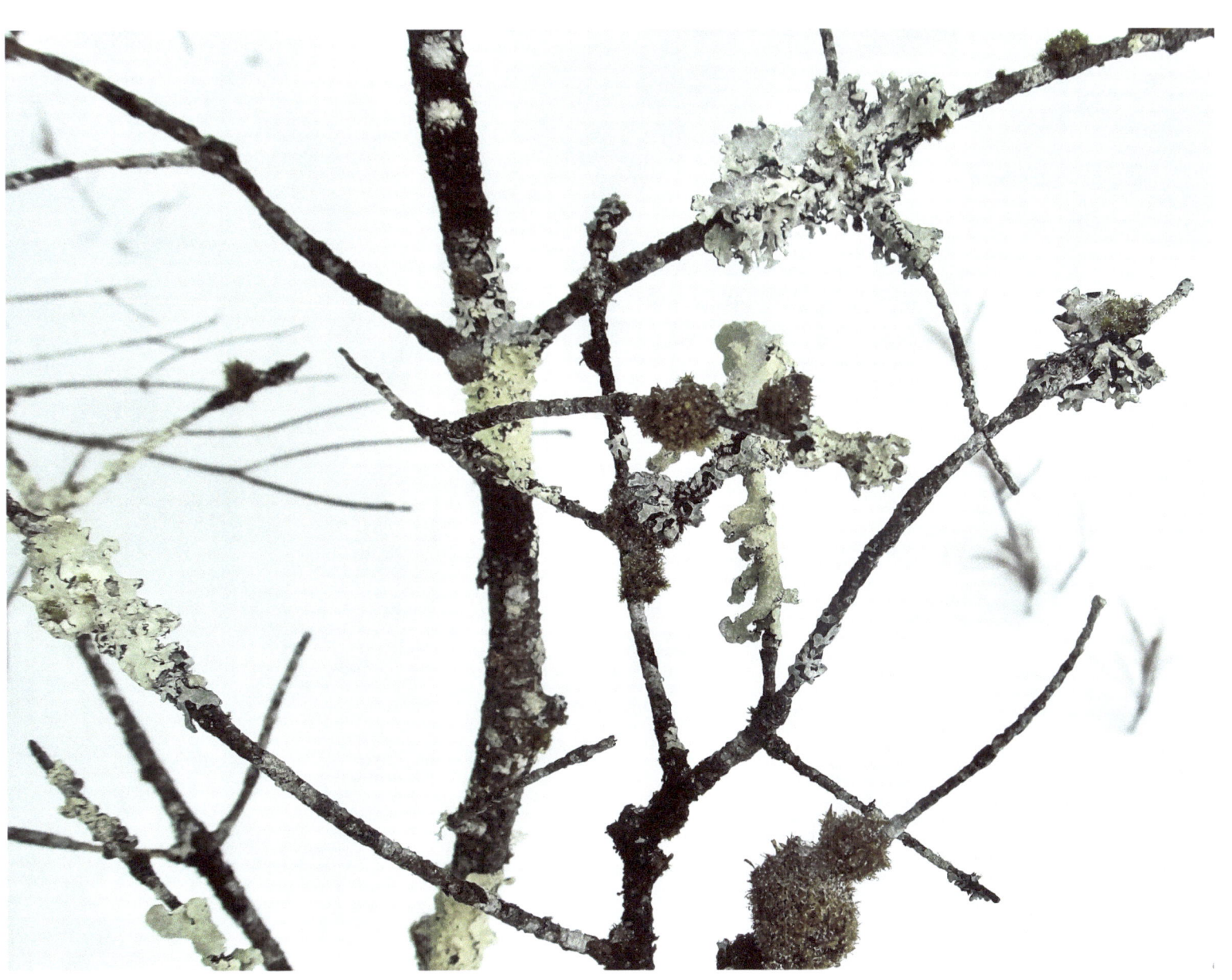

The Forest of Be and Not Be;
or, A Rainy Sunday in December

Snow
hiding the forest floor
where small creatures busily tunnel
safer from the owl.

Warm wind
rolling down the hill
pushing fog and leaving it behind
to smudge contours revealed by snow.

Trunks
black with rain and glaze
reaching starkly from snow volcanoes
pointing out the fog.

Green branches
bearing the season's decorations
of water and ice
turning to water
turning to ice.

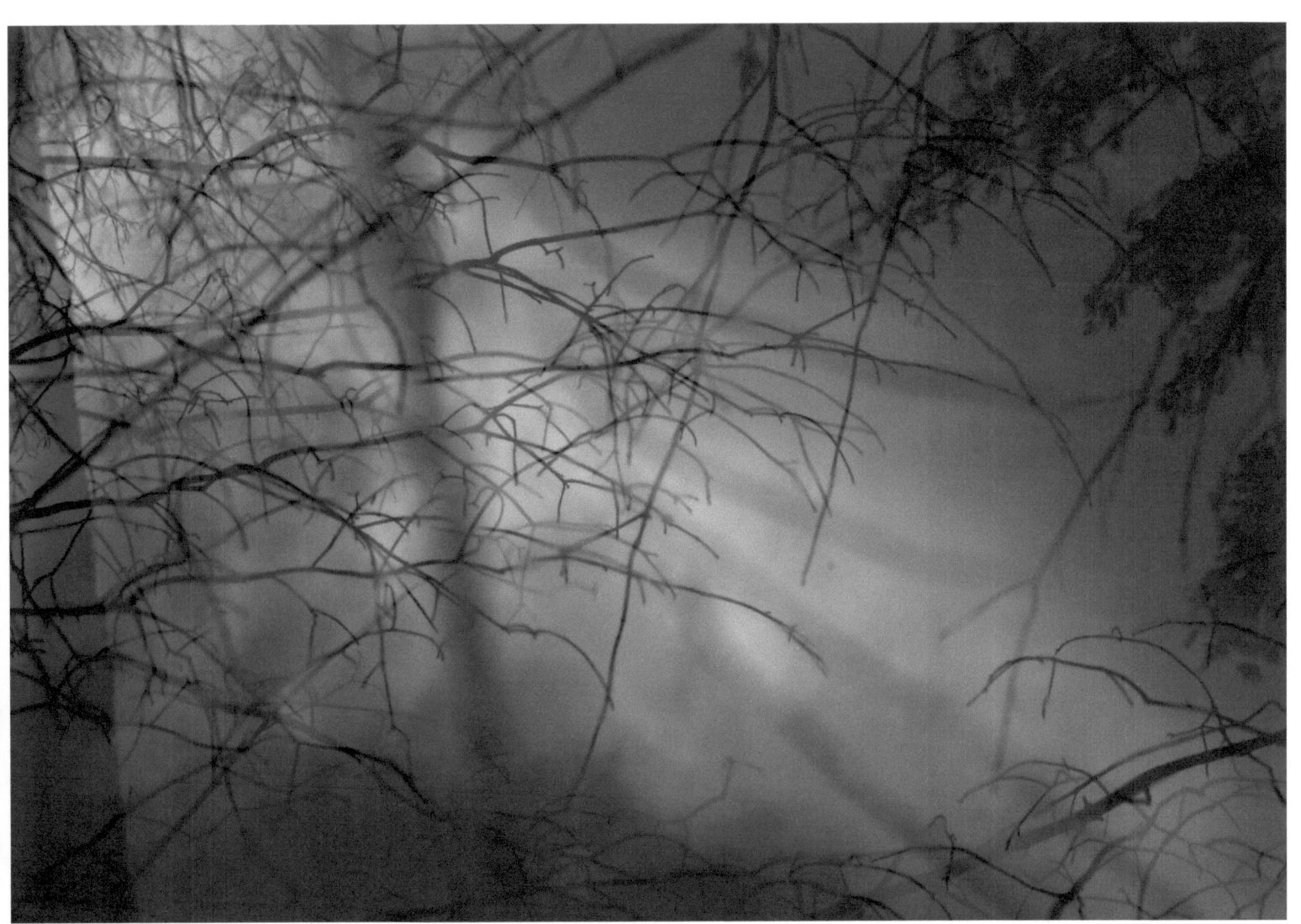

Rats! Forgot to strap on my cleats. Halfway across the road, I look back and stick out my tongue at the front door. I'm tired of all that winter gear. I'll manage.

The forest road is littered with ice fallen down from the trees after the late ice rain. Glittering ice in late February sunshine and the freeze of the clear night. It's some of the best New England has to offer, and sugaring is in full swing.

As I scramble up the road considering what it will be like to try to get back down, I am thinking of Jay, currently engaged in a bike race. The listing on the online leaderboard is "DISTANCE: 1000 DISCIPLINE: Bike Men." It amuses me to no end.

"Following that guy who pushes his bike through the snow for a 1,000 miles in Alaska?" inquired the Carpenter at me, glued to my computer. That one. The Iditarod Trail Invitational. "Bike racers are doing a lot of pushing" in the "pinnacle of all winter ultra-marathons." Some run/walk, some ski, and some bike, and some make it all the way to Nome.

If Jay were to forget a piece of gear and decided not to go back for it, he could be in some serious trouble.

And so might I have been a few weeks ago when the entire forest floor was covered in a thick layer of ice and the daytime temps were in the teens with high winds. Nowhere to go but down and break a leg on the hard ice to boot.

Here lies AgathaO, intrepid dame of a certain age. Harken ye, she was too lazy to get her cleats and perished of hypothermia a mile and a half from her house.

During the winter, a thick layer of compressed and slightly melted snow forms a hard layer of ice under the snow. Evermore water gets packed up in a mini-glaciation event. When the snow melts off, the ice remains. In Alaska or in higher terrain it might not melt during the summer, although of late that's not necessarily been the case.

Add a bit of snow on top and you have the trap we all get in our driveway, writ large. But that winter base of ice is long gone in this crazy season of extremes.

A new layer of snow and ice pieces have made a new crust where the sun hit them. There are a few pockets of stubborn ground ice. I can make it across slippery patches, hoping my boot will stick on emerging small twigs and pieces of rock, doing my penguin walk, setting my heels into the thin layer, and letting momentum take me to the edge of the trail to embrace a tree. Woo-hoo!

The hound is excited by my milling arms and duck walk, jumps up and down and wants to dance. I dance.

We find sticks and throw them. We pull for control of the stick. It's a fine day. Today, everything is possible.

Then I squat down to photograph beech leaves that have melted a pretty snow frame for themselves and it sobers me right up:

This is the way the Arctic is melting: dark water absorbing heat and melting a larger frame for itself.

I've not met Jay. He is married to a climate scientist — my badass friend Nancy — who loves the outdoors as hard as he does. How does she do it? Does she despair every time she sees the world around her with eyes that know what is coming? If so, I don't see it, she's full of forward momentum.

For me, it's my short little span of attention, not to mention the hound's.* There's a new miracle around every corner of every moment: now it's glaciation writ small, and the next moment we're crashing through the ice into a hole because the ground under it swelled with the hard freezes and

was pushed up by the long and irregular funky ice crystals that give ice its power to break mountains.

Now those crystals have collapsed in the melt cycles we've called February this year. If this were an asphalt road, we'd have potholes…

Luckily it isn't and soon we're back up sliding and running and jumping and generally making our way homewards, having had a time of it on this icy hill today. Better than cleats.

Soon it will be spring. Where does the white go when the snow melts?

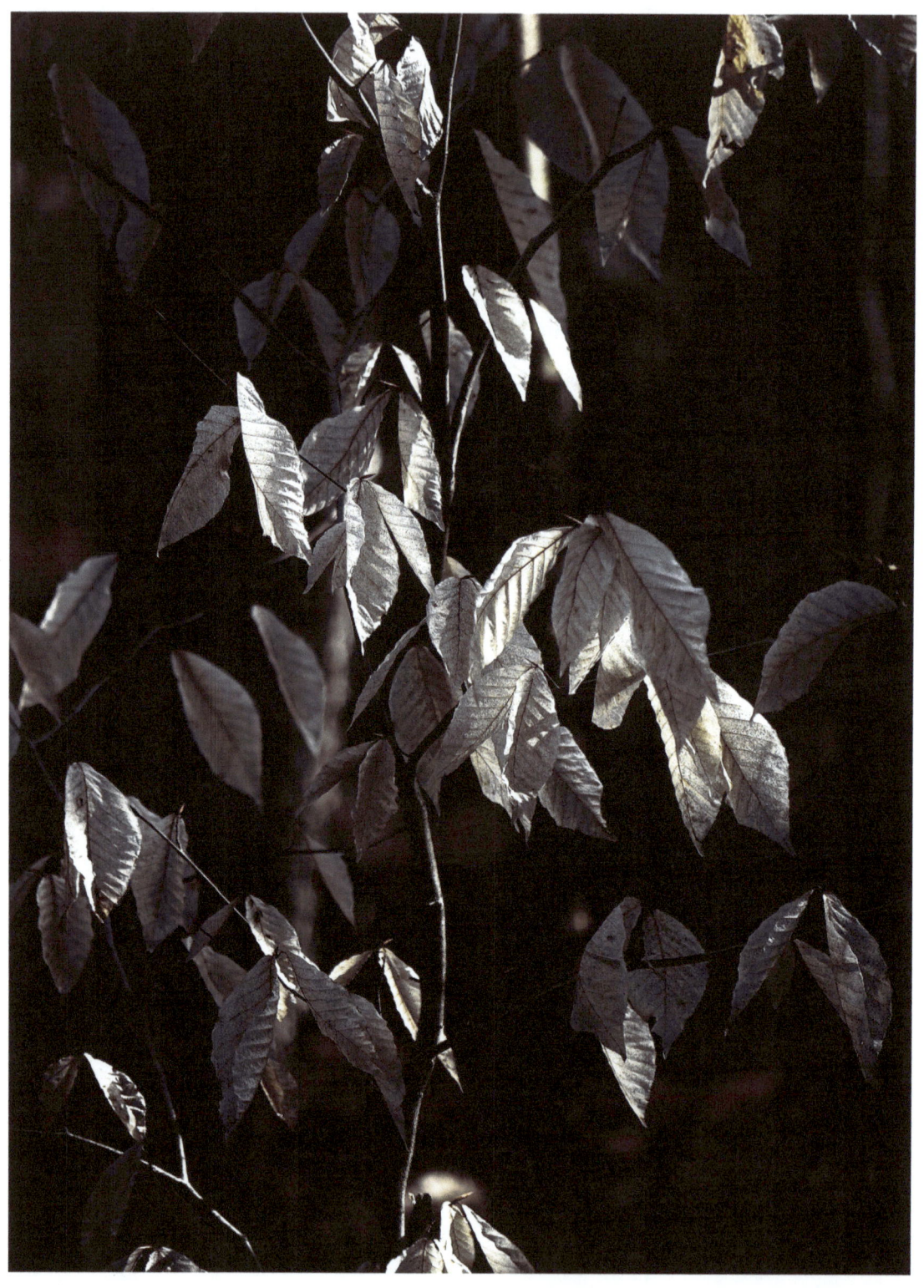

WORKS CITED

Town Plans -- 1830, 1830, no. 20, Plan of Plainfield made by E.S. Darling, November, 1830. SC1/Series 48X. Massachusetts Archives, Boston, Massachusetts. (Accessed 30-12-2018. http://digitalarchives.sec.state.ma.us/uncategorised/digitalFile_2ca963bd-0d7e-41c9-9a1f-fccf6b300692/).

Dillard, Annie, *Pilgrim at Tinker Creek*. New York: Harper's Magazine Press, 1974.

Black, Ralmon. Personal Communication, 2012

Black, Ralmon. "Potash and Asheries: The First and Most Profitable Industry Inroads for Change in the Land; The Industrial Revolution Comes to the Hilltowns. Williamsburg, MA: Williamsburgh Historical Society, 2008. Although Black's is the sole interpretation I have seen that centralizes an industrial/commercial/capitalist extraction of potash in the settlement of the hilltowns, I find his understanding and explanation of the role of potash extraction in the selling, clearing and settlement of the hilltowns to be entirely persuasive.

Bizeau, Michael, and Christine Schultheis. *nature has no boss*. naturehasnoboss.com/about/.

Melville, Herman. *Moby-Dick, Or, The Whale*. New York: Harper and Brothers, 1851.

Haskell, David George. *The Forest Unseen : A Year's Watch in Nature*. New York: Viking, 2012.

Iditarod Trail Invitational
http://www.iditarodtrailinvitational.com/.

"Short little span of attention," from Simon, Paul, "You Can Call Me Al." *Graceland*. Warner Brothers Records 925 447-1, 1986, vinyl. Video: https://www.youtube.com/watch?v=uq-gYOrU8bA (retrieved 1/15/2019).

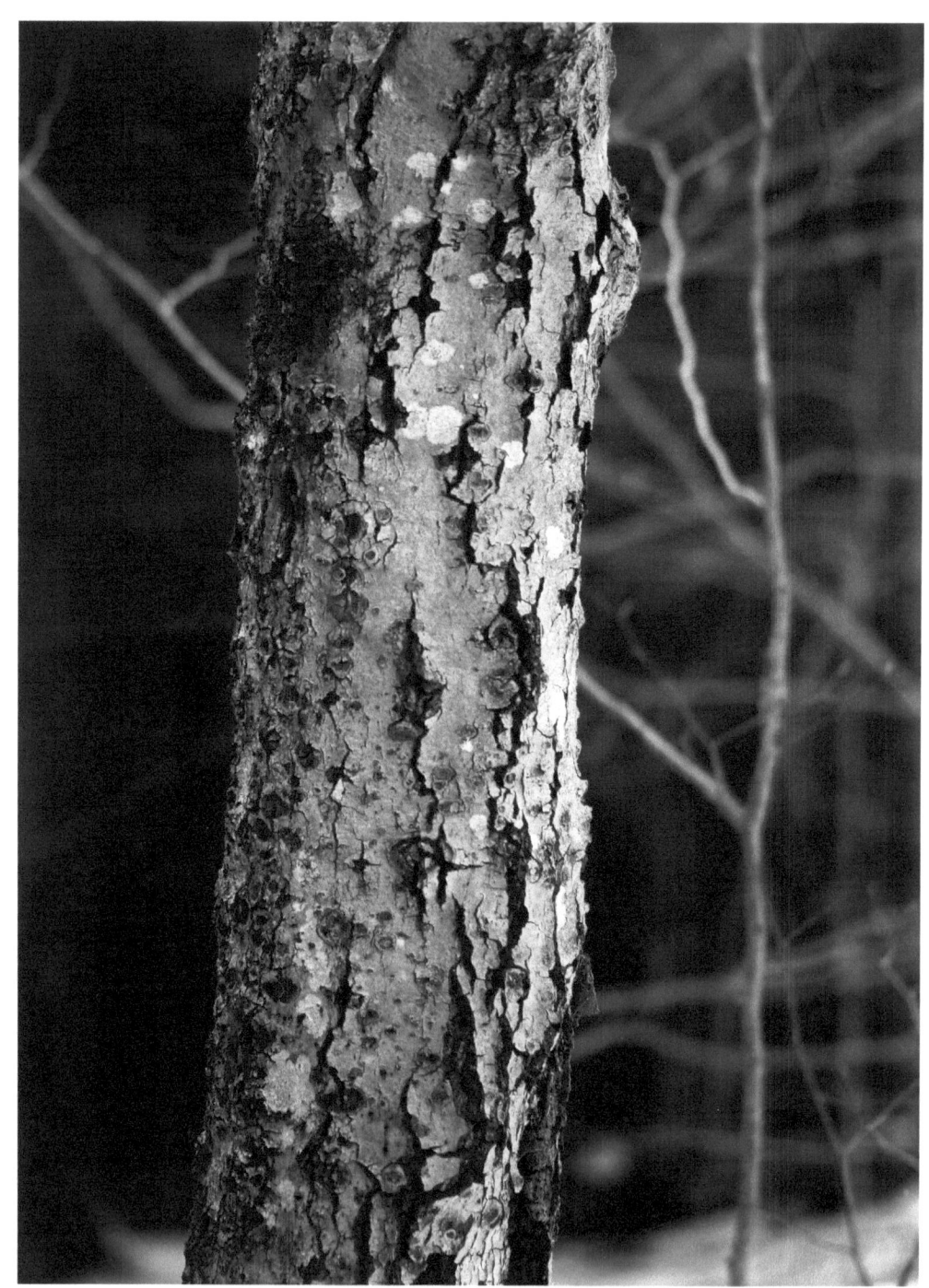

The effects of Beech Bark Disease

ACKNOWLEDGMENTS

Thank you to Tee O'Sullivan for your unflagging encouragement and help, without you no books would be born.

Thank you to the friends who have critiqued, proofread, and in general bore up under the question, "could I just show you three pics and see which one you like best?" Thank you to Mark Roessler for advice; to David Perkins for reading and critiquing an earlier version of this manuscript; and to Erin Miller and Seana Eaton Miller, for providing me with not only a huge lake to help me finish the manuscript, but a kayak to boot. A special thank you to Phil Allessio for walking the forest together lo these many years.

Dedicated to Buddy, who loves his woods almost as much as he does his couch.

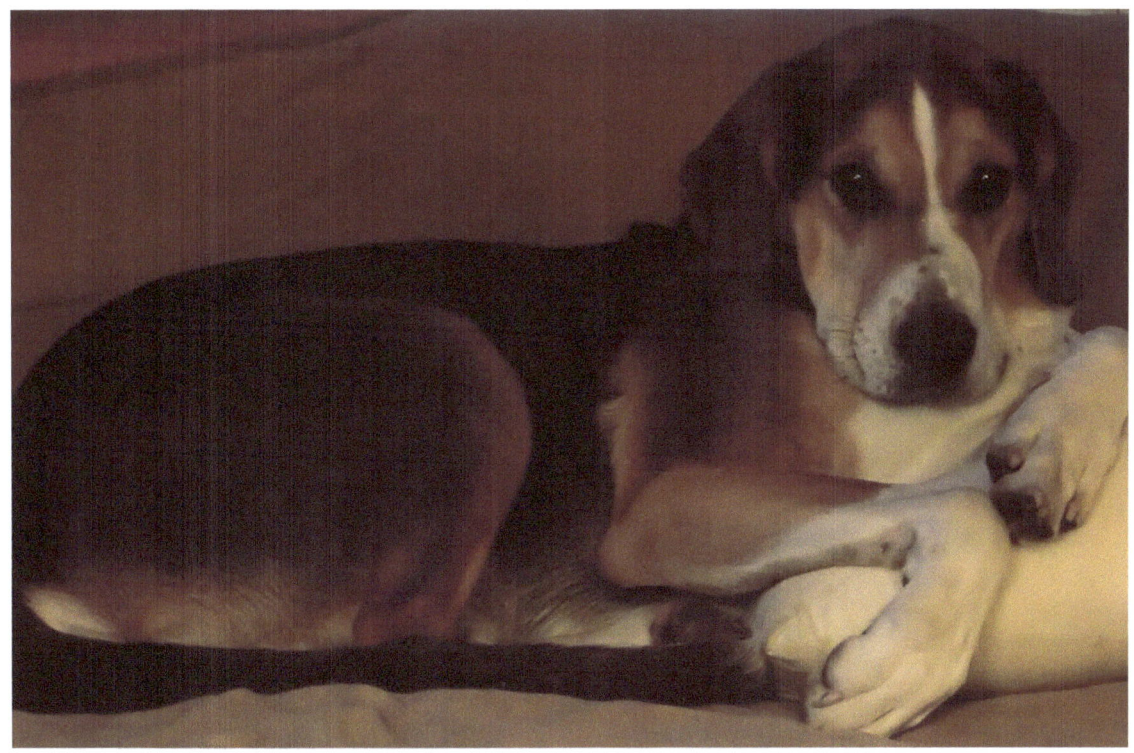

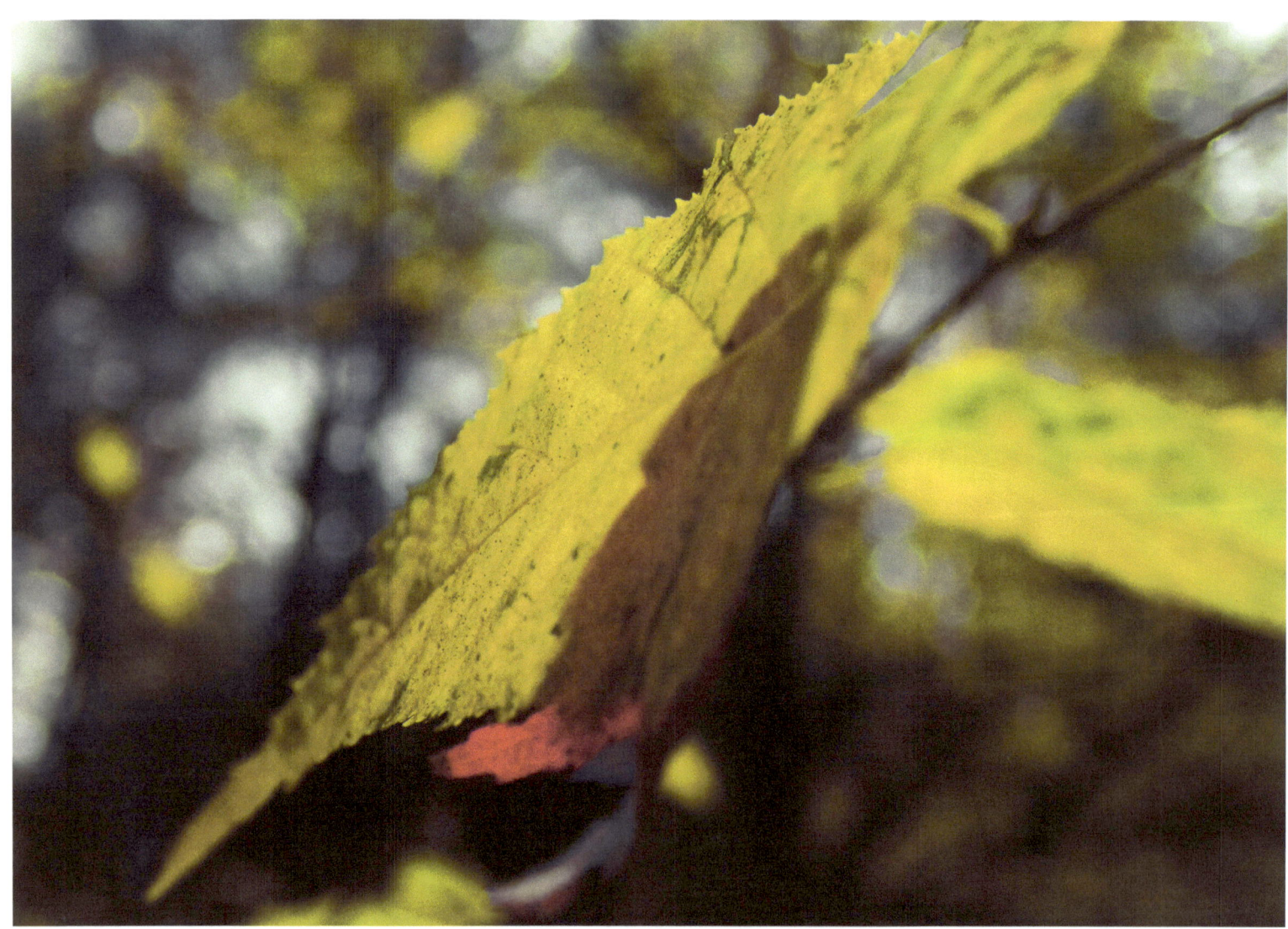

About the Author

AgathaO, an intrepid dame of a certain age, enjoys the adventures of the ordinary, likes to fix what's broken, wants to find out what's what, and has a tendency to drop things and trip and fall into the water.

She is the alter ego of photographer, essayist, historian, and carpenter Pleun Bouricius, who was born and raised in Scheveningen, The Netherlands, and lives in Plainfield, Massachusetts, on a magical forested hillside with a mile of stone walls and a bog, which she calls "three dumps and a swamp."

Pleun graduated from Montclair State College and received a Ph.D. in American Studies from Harvard University. She is the principal of Swift River Press, consulting in public history and communications, and the author of *The Bog* (2017), the website *AgathaO.com*, and the architect and main author *Hidden Walls, Hidden Mills*, a series of history/ecology adventures in Plainfield, MA. She shares her writing and photographs at AgathaO.com